Introduction to
HAIRPIN CROCHET

By the same author:
Hairpin Crochet: Technique and Design (Batsford, 1983)

Introduction to

HAIRPIN CROCHET

PAMELA THOMPSON

B.T. Batsford Ltd
London

Colour photography: Trevor Bray FRPS, AMPA, FRSA Port.
Black and white photography: Nicholas J. Thompson
Line illustrations: Pamela Thompson and Clifford Thompson

ISBN 0 7134 4573 4 (cased)
ISBN 0 7134 4574 2 (limp)

Phototypeset by Tradespools Limited Frome Somerset
and printed in Great Britain by
Anchor Brendon Ltd
Tiptree Essex

for the publishers
B. T. Batsford Ltd.
4 Fitzhardinge Street
London, W1H 0AH

Contents

Acknowledgements

With grateful thanks to my family: to my husband for his help with the illustrations, to my son Nicholas for the black and white photographs, to my daughter Mina for typing and checking the manuscript and to the rest who looked after everything else.

Instructions for working the items in the jacket illustrations

Front jacket

A hairpin, crochet hook and a selection of hairpin braids.
  From the top:
1 The basic braid 1.5 cm (½ in) wide.
2 Guest towel edging (Chapter 8, figure 51).
3 An edging made on a very fine pin (Chapter 15, Using a Victorian hairpin). Work the heading 1 dc 1 ch, into each twisted loop.
4 Tray cloth insertion (Chapter 8, figure 53).
5 Handkerchief edging (Chapter 9, figure 61).

Back jacket

Three decorative bookmarks. Each bookmark requires a 38 cm (15 in) length of ribbon. (Instructions for making up are given in Chapter 15, A Victorian Collection.)
  From the top:
1 Using a basic braid, with a picot heading.
  Materials: 2.5 cm (1 in) wide satin ribbon.
  For the braid, No. 5 perle cotton, 20 mm (¾ in) hairpin, 2.00 crochet hook.
  For the heading, No. 40 crochet cotton, 1.00 crochet hook.
  Method: Make a basic braid having 36 loops.
  Heading. 1 dc into a group of 2 twisted loops, picot using 3 ch, 4 ch.

2 Using motifs as shown in Chapter 11.
  Materials: 3.5 cm (1½ in) wide satin ribbon.
  For the centre motif, No. 5 perle cotton, 15 mm (½ in) hairpin, 2.00 crochet hook.
  For the outer motifs, No. 8 perle cotton, 15 mm (½ in) hairpin, 1.75 crochet hook.
  Work 13 loops for each motif.

3 The bookmark in Chapter 15, figure 100.

Introduction

Hairpin crochet is a charming type of crochet work with light airy characteristics. It is made by the use of two tools, a crochet hook and a hairpin, and any type of yarn ranging from the finest crochet cotton to chunky knitting wools. Victorian ladies used their actual hairpins but hairpin shaped tools are now manufactured in a range of sizes offering the crochet worker a bounty of lacy braids, edgings and insertions.

The different uses to which these hairpin braids can be put seem almost endless. Handkerchief edgings are probably the most popular as their delicate nature is perfect for personal accessories. However, they can be used in many other ways. Home dressmakers can incorporate them as trimmings for collars, cuffs, pockets and hems. Readymade clothing, especially children's wear, can be given the individual look with bright bands of hairpin braids. Household articles can be made elegant, with edgings on table and bed linen, or a cushion appliquéd with chunky woollen braids.

Hairpin crochet, when mastered, is quick to work and economical with yarn. It can be recognised by the loops which are formed down each side of the central crochet and requires knowledge of a few basic crochet stitches which are fully explained. These stitches are then combined with the hairpin to make a very versatile braid. The fascination of hairpin crochet extends beyond the scope of this book in the making of hairpin fabrics which have all the attractive lacy qualities of the simple braids.

About this book

To make hairpin braid it is necessary to learn a few basic crochet stitches before taking up the hairpin. Readers who already know how to crochet are advised to read through the first part to familiarise themselves with the methods used here. This book is divided into three main sections as follows:

Part I teaches the rudiments of crochet work.
Part II introduces the use of a hairpin and shows simple practical uses of the basic braid at each stage.
Part III presents a collection of patterns, each with full working instructions which are based on the techniques learnt in Parts I and II.

Suitable yarns are suggested at each stage during the learning processes. Chapter 6 describes each type of yarn used in the book. Sources of supply for yarns and crochet equipment are listed at the end of the book.

Metric measurements are used throughout the book with the old imperial conversions in brackets.

Abbreviations

Abbreviations are used in the later patterns to avoid the instructions being long and cumbersome. As each stitch is introduced the abbreviation is given in brackets. Here is a complete table:

chain (ch)	group(s) (grp(s))
slip stitch (sl st)	grammes (g)
double crochet (dc)	ounces (oz)
treble (tr)	metre (m)
loop(s) (lp(s))	yard (yd)

Hairpin terms used in the text

loops – the outer loops of a hairpin braid
spine – the central crochet of a hairpin braid

turning chain – one or more chain stitches used at the end of a row ready for the next row

foundation braid – a completed braid ready for further crochet

heading – an additional row of crochet worked into the loops of a foundation braid

group   a number of loops taken up together with one crochet stitch

Hairpin widths

These are also converted from the old imperial measurements to the metric sizes shown below. It will be noticed that the metric hairpin widths offer a more extensive range than the old sizes and in some cases are only approximate equivalents.

10 mm – ½ in   45 mm – 1¾ in
15 mm – ½ in   50 mm – 2 in
20 mm – ¾ in   60 mm – 2½ in
25 mm – 1 in   70 mm – 2¾ in
30 mm – 1¼ in   80 mm – 3 in
35 mm – 1½ in   100 mm – 4 in
40 mm – 1½ in

Yarns and hook sizes

Type of yarn	Metric crochet hook	Old British crochet hook
Mercer crochet 60	0.075 mm	Steel 5
Mercer crochet 40	1.00 mm	Steel 4
Mercer crochet 20	1.25 mm	Steel 3
Mercer crochet 10	1.50 mm	Steel 2½
Perle cotton 8	1.75 mm	Steel 2
Perle cotton 5	2.00 mm	Steel 1 Aluminium 14
Knitting cotton	2.50 mm approx.	Steel 2/0 Aluminium 12
3-ply wool	3.00 mm	Aluminium 11
4-ply wool	3.50 mm	Aluminium 9
Craft cotton Dishcloth cotton	3.50 mm or 4.00 mm	Aluminium 9 or 10
Double knitting wool	4.00 mm or 4.50 mm	Aluminium 8 or 7
Aran types	5.00 mm	Aluminium 6
Chunky wools	5.50 mm	Aluminium 5

This chart is for guidance as the bulk of any type of yarn can vary between different brands. Also different workers produce different tensions, so adjust the size of hook to give a satisfactory stitch by working a short sample chain first.

For American readers

The following tables show the American equivalents for the crochet stitch terms and abbreviations, and suggested hook sizes for the range of yarns used in this book.

Crochet stitch conversion

British	*American*
chain (ch)	chain (ch)
slip stitch (sl st)	slip st (sl st)
double crochet (dc)	single crochet (sc)
treble (tr)	double crochet (dc)

Yarns and hook sizes

Mercer crochet 60	Steel 12
Mercer crochet 40/30	Steel 9
Mercer crochet 20	Steel 8
Mercer crochet 10/ Knit-Cro-Sheen	Steel 7
Perle cotton 8	Steel 6
Perle cotton 5	B 1
Knitting cotton	C 2
3 ply wool	D 3
4 ply wool	E 4
Craft/ dish cloth cotton	F 5
Double knitting wool	G 6
Aran types	H 8

I

LEARNING
TO CROCHET

1 Getting ready

What is crochet? Crochet is one of the most versatile of all yarn crafts in that it can be narrow or wide, can form almost any shape, round, square, rectangular, triangular, and can be worked directly onto a fabric into which a crochet hook can be inserted.

The word 'crochet' is derived from the French 'croche' which means hook and gives the tool used its name. The basis of crochet work is the drawing of a loop through a loop by using the hook. It is a simple process and quickly mastered provided that the student obtains suitable equipment and is prepared to take care with the groundwork.

Equipment and materials

Crochet hooks

These cover a large range of sizes from a very fine steel hook for use with the finest cotton yarns to a chunky, aluminium hook for the thick knitting wools. New hooks are now manufactured in metric sizes which will be quoted throughout this book but the old British size hooks are likely to be in circulation for some time so for those who already have these hooks figure 1 shows the new metric sizes above and the equivalent old British sizes below covering the whole range of sixteen sizes.

Choose good quality hooks which feel comfortable and well balanced when held as one holds a pencil, and of a smooth finish so that the hook will pass easily through the yarn. Using cheap tools that are likely to snag the yarn will only lead to frustration.

Yarns

Almost any type of yarn can be used for crochet and modern manufacturers provide a very wide range from which to choose.

Knitting yarns are constantly changing using wool, cotton, synthetics and mixtures of these, whilst older yarns are discontinued. Retail outlets cannot possibly stock all the ranges, so the

2/0 ALUMINIUM 12

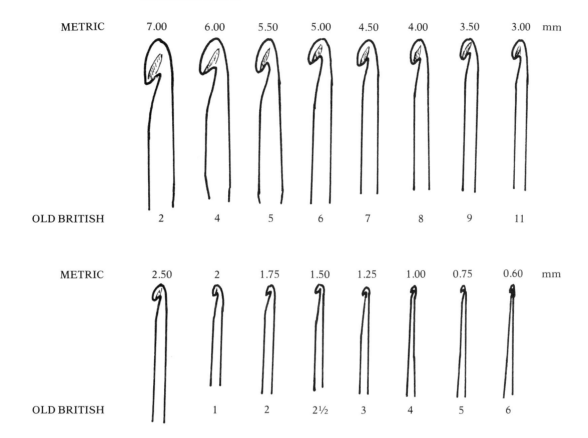

METRIC	7.00	6.00	5.50	5.00	4.50	4.00	3.50	3.00	mm
OLD BRITISH	2	4	5	6	7	8	9	11	

METRIC	2.50	2	1.75	1.50	1.25	1.00	0.75	0.60	mm
OLD BRITISH		1	2	2½	3	4	5	6	

1 The complete range of crochet hooks. Actual size.

patterns in this book quote the type of yarn only, i.e. 4 ply, double knitting, Aran etc.

Crochet cottons remain fairly constant. Mercerised cottons in the most popular thickness are No. 10 (the thickest), 20, 40 and 60. The latter is quite fine; 80 and 100 are available for exceedingly fine work but are not featured in this book.

Other types of yarn which are suitable for hairpin crochet are discussed in Chapter 6.

Recommendations for the beginner

The beginner should select a yarn that is smooth and firm allowing the hook to glide through it. A light colour is advisable so that it is easy to see the formation of the stitches. I suggest double knitting wool of a light colour with a firm twist. Crepe wool is ideal as it does not split easily.

Crochet hook size 4.00 mm (old size 8) comes in the middle of the crochet hook size range, is comfortable to hold, and will produce a stitch that can easily be seen.

15

To many people crochet means intricate edgings, doylies and Duchesse sets made in fine cotton using a tiny hook, worked at speed by their older relations. The enthusiastic beginner may feel disappointed to find that their first steps in crochet are to be made with a comparatively clumsy hook and thick wool, but these are easy to hold and will produce a large stitch which will enable the worker to compare the structure of the stitch with the relevant diagram. Opportunity to use finer yarns is provided at the end of Part I when the worker will be familiar with the working of crochet.

$\underline{\overline{2}}$ Starting to learn

This chapter shows the beginner how to hold the hook and yarn in a comfortable and efficient manner, and then gives step-by-step instructions for making a slip knot and a chain.

Before you start

The learning scheme is set out as follows:
1 A general description of the work in hand.
2 The detailed instructions are set well spaced from other matter so that the eye can easily see the instructions whilst actually working. This stage is supported by illustrations so that by reading and seeing you can understand the working process.
3 Solutions for any likely problems which may have arisen are listed for those in difficulty.

Left-handed readers will, as usual, read left for right but may become a little bemused when following the diagrams, especially in the first part. In this case it may help to make a tracing of the diagrams and then turn it over.

Organise your working conditions well by sitting at a table with good light and the book in front of you. Have your yarn feeding smoothly from your left in a container on the floor. Now you are ready to begin.

Holding the hook

Most crochet hooks have a flattened area on the shaft where the hook can be held like a pencil with the right hand. When held in this position, the shaft will not roll whilst in use and the hook will be turned to the left which is the correct position for taking up the crochet loops (figure 2).

Making a slip knot

When starting to crochet, a loop is placed on the hook and this is made by a slip knot which can be adjusted to the size of the hook. It is made as follows:

2 Holding the crochet hook.

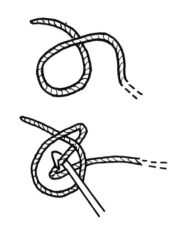

1 Hold the yarn in the left hand approx. 5 cm (2 in) from the cut end.

2 With the right hand take the long end down and round to make a loose ring crossing over where the yarn is held in the left hand (figure 3a). The thumb and first finger can now hold the ring where the yarn crosses.

3 Take up the hook and insert it through the ring, and catch the long end. Draw the hook back towards you pulling the loop through (figure 3b).

4 Hold both ends of the yarn to tighten the knot. Adjust the loop on the hook by pulling on the long end so that the loop fits easily.

3a 3b Making a slip knot.

Holding the yarn

It is essential that the yarn is held correctly so that it can move freely through the fingers but without slackness. A correct holding position will also avoid cramped fingers and is necessary to achieve a good tension. Remove the hook from the slip knot temporarily whilst mastering the holding technique.

1 Hold the slip knot with the thumb and first finger of the left hand. The short end hangs in front of the fingers. The long end lies over the first and second fingers, under the fourth and behind the fifth (figure 4).

2 At this stage the yarn feels sloppy and the fingers will only have minimal control. To correct this the yarn is hooked onto the little finger as follows: take hold of the yarn where it lies between the third and fourth finger arrowed in figure 4. Pull slightly towards you, then hook the yarn onto the little finger. The long end now leaves at the base of the little finger (figure 5).

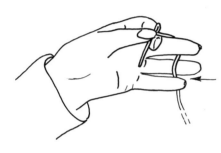

4 Holding the yarn.

This process may seem tedious but is worth a little perseverance. If the yarn is simply wound around the little finger with the long end leaving near the tip it will keep slipping off.

The fingers will now feel able to control the yarn. Pull the long end and then open the fingers slightly to feel the tension. Repeat this a few times and then insert the hook back into the slip knot ready to make the first chain stitch.

Working the chain stitch (ch)

The chain stitch is the basis of all crochet stitches. Holding the slip knot firmly, check that the yarn position is correct. Check that the hook is held correctly, the slip knot should sit in the hook neatly but should be large enough to slide up the shaft. Study figure 6 noting that the hook is lying to the left of the yarn which bridges the first and second fingers.

5 Hooking the yarn round the little finger.

1 To work the chain stitch, pass the hook from left to right under the yarn (as arrowed in figure 6) catching it in the hook.

2 Draw the hook back towards you and through the slip loop (figure 7). The first chain stitch is now complete.

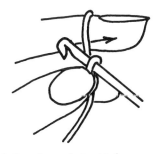

6 Starting a chain stitch.

7 Completing a chain stitch.

3 Repeat this process to make a long chain continually moving the thumb and first finger up to their position just under the loop on the hook. This will ensure that you are always in control. The loop on the hook should be fairly slack, it should never have to be dragged through. Figure 8 shows the position of the hands when working a chain.

At first there may be a tendency to work tightly so it is advisable to practise a long chain until the action of the hook is smooth and rhythmic, with the yarn passing easily through the fingers of the left hand. Practise until the chain stitches are of even size.

Obviously the beginner will not start and finish the whole of Part I in one session. When taking up the work after a break it is advisable to revise the techniques already mastered before going forward to the next lesson.

8 Working a foundation chain.

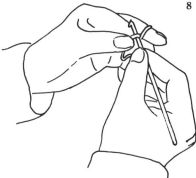

3 Making a sampler

This is purely a practice piece and should be kept for future reference. There are two methods by which a piece of crochet can be made:

1 By working into each stitch of a chain along its length, turning the work at the end and working back again as in knitting.
2 By joining a chain to form a ring and then working round and round without turning.

Important

At each numbered stage read the instructions to the end before starting work. Study the appropriate illustrations and try to visualise the whole process. When working, constantly refer to the figure as well as the written instructions. Make sure the position of yarn and tools is exactly as shown.

The foundation chain

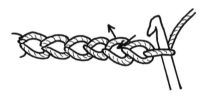

9 Inserting the hook into a chain stitch.

The chain is now used as a base for a second row of crochet stitches and is called a foundation chain. Lay your length of chain down flat to see a distinct chain effect down one side as in figure 9. Now turn it over to note that each chain has an extra thread down the middle. When working into the chain the plain chain must face you all the time; it may tend to twist a little. For the sampler, work a new foundation chain having 20 stitches. As the next row will be worked into this chain it is essential that the crochet hook can be inserted easily. Check this; if there is any tightness work a slacker chain.

The double crochet stitch (dc)

All crochet stitches are an extension of the chain stitch. Begin with six rows of double crochet. Work from right to left along the foundation chain as follows:
1 Insert the hook into the second chain from the hook as shown

10 The chain stitch on the hook.

11 Catching the yarn to draw through the first loop.

12 Catching the yarn to draw through two loops.

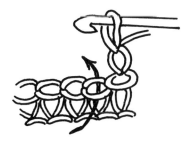

14 The turning chain.

15 Working a second row of double crochet.

by the arrows on figure 9. Now there are two loops on the hook (figure 10).

2 Catch the yarn exactly like working the chain stitch then draw it back through the first loop on the hook only as shown by the arrows on figure 11. Again you will have two loops on the hook.

3 Catch the yarn again and draw it through both loops together (figure 12). The double crochet is now complete, having used the chain process twice to make one double crochet (figure 13). Continue along the whole length of the foundation chain.

Keep an easy tension making sure you work into each stitch of the foundation chain. Sometimes the chain next to that being worked is pulled smaller; look carefully for each stitch. Always keep control by holding the work under the hook as described for the chain stitch.

Correcting mistakes

When pulling back after a mistake keep hold of the yarn in the left hand, unravel as far as necessary, then take up the slack by pulling the yarn below the little finger.

double crochet

foundation chain

13 The completed double crochet.

The turning chain

On reaching the end of the row, work one chain. This is the turning chain which also makes the first stitch of the second row. Note the chain which lies along the top of the double crochet (figure 14). The work is now turned but the chain lying on top of the dc is not as visible from this side so tip the edge towards you a little. Study figure 15 to see that the turning chain stands on top of the last double crochet of the first row. The next double crochet will therefore be worked into the third chain from the hook as arrowed. You will also see the arrow takes up both loops of the chain so the double crochet is now worked as follows:

1 Insert the hook under the two loops of the double crochet, catch the yarn and draw through the first two loops on the hook.

2 Catch the yarn and draw through both loops on the hook.

The double crochet is now worked in this manner except when worked into a foundation row.

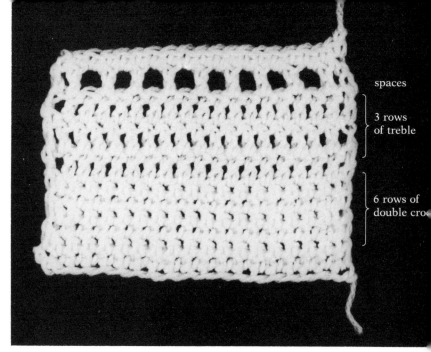

spaces

3 rows
of treble

6 rows of
double cro[c]

16 A crochet sampler.

Continue in this way to the end of the row, chain one and turn. Make sure you work into the very last stitch which is the turning chain of the previous row. It is sometimes difficult to find as it may look like a small knot so give the hook a firmer push. If the sampler starts to decrease you will have missed the last stitch. There should be 19 double crochet stitches on each row. Work about six rows to give a neat close fabric (figure 16).

Other uses of double crochet
This is a versatile stitch which can be worked straight onto other fabrics. The fabric replaces the foundation chain, an obvious example being a hemstitched handkerchief where a double crochet is worked into the holes. It is also frequently used to edge a knitted fabric.

17 Working a treble.

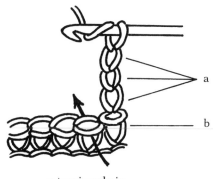

a turning chain

b last dc of previous row

22

The treble stitch (tr)
This is the second stitch used on the sampler. It is a longer stitch, a further extension of the double crochet which is achieved by making an extra loop at the beginning. The turning chain must now match the length of the treble, so at the end of the last row of double crochet work three chains. Turn the work ready for making the first treble. Study figure 17 before starting.
1 Catch the yarn in the hook to make an extra loop. Insert the hook into the fifth chain from the hook (the second double crochet from the end) as arrowed. Catch the yarn and draw through two loops. There will now be three loops on the hook.
2 Catch the yarn and draw through two loops, the second of those being the extra loop made at the beginning.

18 The treble completed.

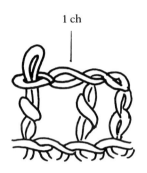

1 ch

19 Making spaces.

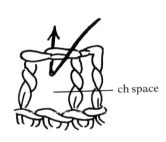

ch space

20 Crocheting into a space.

3 Catch the yarn and draw through the remaining two loops. The treble is now complete (figure 18).

There may be a tendency for the extra loop to twist forward when working stage 2 but this is easily pushed back.

Repeat into each double crochet to the end of the row working the last treble into the top of the turning chain (19 stitches). Work two more treble rows in the same manner.

This is a pleasing stitch to work as it creates a smooth rhythm and is used in the making of open lacy patterns.

Making spaces

The last part of the sampler shows a row of spaces. This is not a new stitch but simply an arrangement of all the stitches now mastered. The spaces are made by working a treble into each alternate treble of the previous row. A chain stitch is worked between each treble to bridge the space along the top edge (figure 19).

Reading abbreviations

The instructions for the two final rows are given in abbreviated form as follows:
chain (ch), double crochet (dc), treble (tr).

At the end of the last tr row work 3 ch, turn.
1 tr into next tr of previous row.
*1 ch, miss 1 tr, 1 tr into the next tr. Repeat from *to the end of the row, 1 tr into the top of the turning ch, 1 ch, turn (8 spaces).

Compare with figure 16. There are two trebles side by side at each end of the row.

The final row

This is a row of double crochet which gives a firm, neat finish. A double crochet is worked into the top of each treble. It is, however, difficult to work into the single chain stitches so here work the double crochet into the chain space by inserting the hook under the chain (figure 20).

1 dc into the 2nd tr, *1 dc into the next ch space, 1 dc into the next tr. Repeat from *to the end of the row. 1 dc into the top of the turning ch.

Finishing off

Leaving approximately 3.5 cm (1½ in) cut the yarn, draw through the loop and tighten. Loose ends are run in with a bodkin.

4 Making a motif

21 A crochet motif.

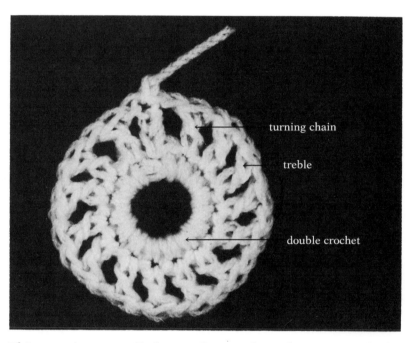

turning chain

treble

double crochet

This exercise uses all the stitches used in Chapter 3 with the addition of a slip stitch. The motif starts with a short foundation chain which is joined into a ring by means of the very simple slip stitch. Two rounds of crochet are then built upon the ring (figure 21).

The slip stitch (sl st)

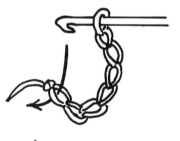

Work seven chain stitches, insert the hook into the first chain (figure 22a). Catch the yarn, thereby drawing both ends together, and draw through both the loops on the hook. The slip stitch is now made and will be used to join all successive rounds (figure 22b).

22a 22b Making a slip stitch.

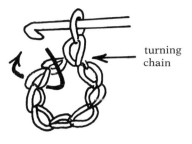

23 Working into a ring.

turning chain

The motif

The first round is of double crochets, the second of trebles. Although the work is not turned as for the sampler a turning chain is used to bring the hook up into position and it also stands as the first double crochet (figure 23).

The first round of double crochet
Study figure 21 to identify the first round of double crochet which shows a strong neat ring.
1 After making the ring with a slip stitch, work 1 chain stitch.
2 Work 14 double crochets side by side into the ring as arrowed on figure 23. This may look impossible but by working the stitches very close together (and taking care not to cover the turning chain) the 14th double crochet will lie next to the turning chain.
3 To complete the round join the 14th double crochet to the turning chain with a slip stitch.

The second round using trebles
As the circumference of this round will be greater than the first round, provision is made by working 1 chain stitch between each treble.
1 Make 3 chain stitches which stand as a treble.
2 Work 1 treble into the next double crochet, 1 chain. Repeat to the end of the round.
3 Make a slip stitch into the top of the turning chain having made 15 trebles including the turning chain. Fasten off.

Using crochet cotton

As many of the patterns in this book use crochet cotton for finer edgings it will be worthwhile repeating this motif with a smaller hook and finer yarn. The instructions for the motif are now given in abbreviated form. Use a 1.50 mm hook and No.10 crochet cotton.

Ch 7, join into a ring with a sl st.
First round: 1 ch, 14 dc into the ring, join with a sl st.
Second round: 3 ch, *1 tr into the next dc, 1 ch. Repeat from *to the end of the round, join with a sl st to the top of the 3 ch. Finish off.

The rudiments of crochet work are now complete for the purpose of this book, and the techniques acquired sufficient to carry forward into Part II. The reader may, by now, have had a glimpse of all the exciting possibilities to be found with hook and yarn.

It may, however, be sensible to pause and assess your own

progress. Do you work with a pleasing, regular rhythm? Can you identify the different stitches and know exactly where to insert the hook? Does the finished product look neat and even? Should you be doubtful on any of these points it would be wise either to repeat the sampler and the motif or, if this seems unproductive, to find one of many excellent crochet books to be found in bookshops and libraries, or pattern leaflets, and choose a simple motif. These are fun to do using oddments of wool and can be joined together to make cushion covers and blankets. Likewise find a pattern for a simple edging for a handkerchief or pillow case.

When choosing a pattern, look for a good photograph of the finished article together with a clear close-up view to refer to in conjunction with the written instructions.

Working a larger project will give valuable experience both in handling and pattern reading. Remember, practice makes perfect.

II

LEARNING
HAIRPIN CROCHET

$\overline{\underline{5}}$ Working hairpin crochet

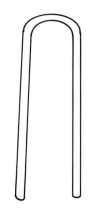

24 A modern hairpin.

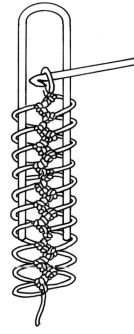

25 Working the basic braid.

Now that the worker is familiar with crochet, this second part shows how the crochet hook, yarn and stitches are combined with the hairpin to produce an appealing range of braids.

The hairpin tool

This is not so much a tool in that it does not do anything complicated but acts as a frame around which the crochet is worked. Modern hairpins for crochet are made in a range of widths from 10.00 mm (½ in) to 100 mm (4 in) (see page 11 for the complete range). They are manufactured in a lightweight alloy and stockists of knitting equipment may have them in stock or would be willing to order them. Figure 24 shows the 20 mm (¾ in) size, its actual length being 13 cm (5 in). This pin features in a large proportion of the patterns in this book and is ideal for the beginner as it is easy to hold.

Hooks and yarns

To start with, these will be as used in Part I. The yarn always determines the size of the hook, the hairpin merely governs the width of the braid. A quick look through the book shows that eventually it is possible to make both wool and cotton braids in any width according to their purpose.

How it is done

Study figure 25 to see that the crochet stitches lie in the centre of the hairpin with the yarn wrapped around both prongs. The crochet stitches used here are the chain and double crochet and by turning the pin over after each 'row' the yarn is taken around the prongs. As the braid grows it comes off the pin at the open end, to show the loops at each side of the braid which are unique to hairpin crochet.

With the open end down, hold the empty pin between the thumb and first finger of the left hand. The fingers should be

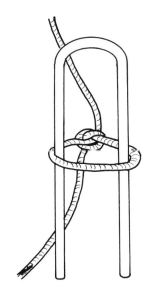

26 The slip loop on the hairpin.

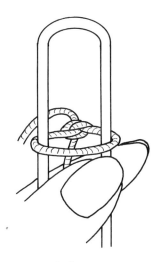

27 Holding the hairpin.

about halfway down the pin as the crochet will be worked in the upper half. The only action the pin makes is a turn from right to left. Holding the hook and yarn is exactly as before, so in reality the hairpin is part of the crochet. There will perhaps be some clumsiness to start with but a little patience and practice will soon cure this. Once the technique is mastered, the work grows very quickly and is very rewarding.

Assemble your equipment: double knitting wool, a 4.00 (old size 8) hook and a 20 mm (¾ in) hairpin.

Remember the working rules set down at the beginning of Chapter 3: before starting read through each numbered stage to the end and refer to the appropriate illustration; whilst working constantly compare your own work with the illustrations.

Making the first loop (lp(s))

In order to start crocheting a hairpin braid, it is necessary to 'cast on' so that there is a loop around each prong of the hairpin with a stitch in the centre (as illustrated in figure 30). This is achieved as follows:

1 Make a slip knot large enough to slip over both prongs of the hairpin. Adjust the loop to fit firmly with the knot at the centre back (figure 26).
2 Take the hairpin, open end down, between the thumb and first finger of the left hand. Hold the hook and long end of the yarn in the normal crocheting position, the short end held firmly with the thumb (figure 27).
3 Pass the hook underneath the loop round the prongs and catch the yarn (figure 28).
4 Draw the hook towards you then over the loop on the prong to catch the yarn (figure 29). Work one chain. The casting on is now complete (figure 30).

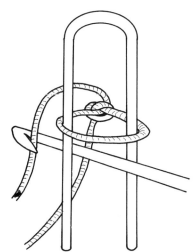

28 Casting on: passing the hook under the loop.

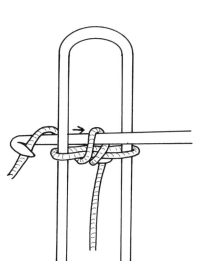

29 Drawing the yarn back over the loop.

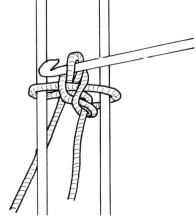

30 The first stitch completed.

29

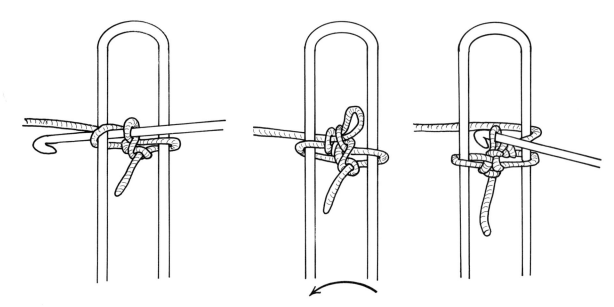

31 Starting a double crochet into the left loop.

32 The double crochet complete.

33 After turning the hairpin.

Crocheting the basic braid

The crochet at the centre of the braid is very simple, consisting of one chain and one double crochet.

1 The first double crochet. Insert the hook into the front of the left loop (figure 31). Work one double crochet, i.e. catch the yarn, draw it back towards you, take it over the top of the loop to catch the yarn again and draw it through the loops on the hook (figure 32).

2 Remove the hook from the stitch and turn the hairpin over from right to left as shown by the arrow on figure 32. At this stage allow the yarn in the left hand to run easily so as not to pull the stitch back. After completing the turn the yarn will be wrapped around the prong on the right (figure 33).

3 Insert the hook back into the stitch, then catch the yarn to make one chain. Figure 25 shows the work at this stage.

Repeat stages 1, 2 and 3 until the tension is even. It can easily be remembered as '1 ch, 1 dc into the front left loop, turn'. Fasten off after the double crochet.

Taking the hook out of the stitch may seem tedious at first but after practice this will become part of a regular rhythm, and the braid will grow quickly. When the braid is removed from the pin, notice the slight elastic quality which enables it to form curves quite easily. It often shows to a better effect when it is slightly stretched. This is the simplest version of hairpin crochet, called the basic braid, and is now ready for use in a variety of ways.

6 Basic braids with different yarns

34 Three examples of basic braid, reading from the top:
20 mm (¾ in) wide made with double knitting wool.
15 mm (½ in) wide made with a 4 ply yarn.
15 mm (½ in) wide made with a perle cotton No. 8.

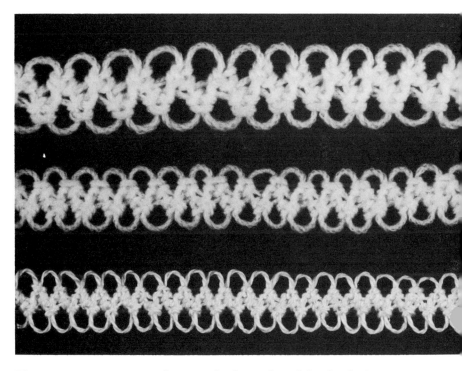

There are many ways of using the basic braid for both decorative and practical purposes. Figure 34 illustrates how the scope widens further when the braid is made with different types of yarn and different widths. Before progressing any further with the hairpin it will be worthwhile stopping to look at the properties of knitting yarns and crochet cottons featured in the rest of this book.

Yarn types

Knitting yarns
Manufacturers are constantly changing their products and retail outlets selling certain ranges may be difficult to find so the

patterns do not give brand names but quote the type of yarn only. These range from chunky (the thickest), double knitting, 4 ply and baby wool (the finest).

Crochet cottons

These ranges remain fairly constant and are stocked at most knitting and embroidery shops. They come in several thicknesses and attractive colours and two main types.

Mercerised cottons

Mercerised crochet cottons are the most popular. They are tightly spun and are very hard wearing. The thickest is No. 10, already mentioned in Chapter 4. The higher the number the finer the thread, therefore Nos. 10 and 20 are used for household linens. No. 40 makes finer edgings for handkerchiefs and other dainty articles. Nos. 60, 80 and even 100 are available but are not used in this book.

Perle cottons

Perle cottons are soft and loosely spun with a silky sheen and can be found in most needlework shops stocking Anchor or D M C yarns. They are mostly available in balls of No. 5 (the thickest) and No. 8, and are beautiful for decorative braids giving the effect of rich embroidery. Do not confuse this type of perle cotton with a perle knitting yarn which some manufacturers are now making.

Knitting and crochet cottons

These are a thicker version of the mercerised crochet cottons and are very hard wearing. They come under the brand names of Lysbet by Twilleys and Knitting and Crochet cotton No. 6 by Anchor, but unfortunately are not easy to find. They can be ordered by post from the stockists listed at the end of the book.

Other yarns more of the novelty type are used in just a few patterns, so these will be described along with the instructions. These include string, lurex, dishcloth cotton and Raffene.

Choosing yarns

Yarns should be chosen with care if the article on which they are used needs frequent washing, especially with the woollen types where there may be shrinkage, so where possible do not mix natural yarns with synthetics.

When working on your own projects be guided by the following facts. As it is the loops which make the braid so attractive and unusual avoid choosing a floppy yarn or one too fine for the required width of the braid, otherwise the loops will twist and look straggly and the crocheting will be limp. As hairpin crochet is economical with yarn it is a good idea to look in the oddment boxes in wool shops as these are often very much reduced in price; one ball will make a lot of braid.

$\overline{7}$ How to use the basic braid

35 A decorative braid on a jumper.

The three braids in figure 34 are now put to practical use. Each one is described in detail, then there are general working instructions including methods of applying them to fabrics.

The stretch (or tension) figures are given as a guide to help the worker assess the length of braid required for the work in hand.

A decorative braid (figure 35)

This is the braid used in practice, i.e. 20 mm (¾ in) wide using double knitting wool and a 4.00 mm hook.

It is shown here worked in black wool applied above the welt of a white sweater. The tips of the loops are stitched down with red wool. Here is an opportunity to have fun with bright colours

36 An edging braid in wool.

especially on children's wear such as on the bib of dungarees or round the hem of a skirt.

Stretch to 2½ loops per 2.5 cm (1 in).

An edging braid in wool (figure 36)

This is a very useful braid for edging a jacket or a knitted cardigan, and is comparatively cheap to make.

It is made on a 15 mm (½ in) hairpin using a 3.50 mm hook and 4 ply yarn which results in a more compact braid which will conceal the raw edge of a single hem. Place the outer loops exactly on the edge. Made in either toning or contrasting yarn, it will give an elegant result.

Stretch to 3 loops per 2.5 cm (1 in).

A half edging braid in perle cotton (figure 37)

This is a narrow decorative edging shown here on a wide dress sleeve. The loops on the outer side lie beyond the sleeve edge.

Use a 10 mm or 15 mm (½ in) hairpin, a 1.75 mm hook with perle cotton No. 8. The home dressmaker can use this braid on pockets, collars, and for seam detail. When used in a matching cotton the sheen on this type of cotton looks very distinctive.

Stretch to 5 loops per 2.5 cm (1 in).

Calculating the length of braid

The instructions state the estimated number of loops per 2.5 cm (1 in) when stretched and ready for stitching down. Adjustments may be necessary depending on the type of yarn or the tension of

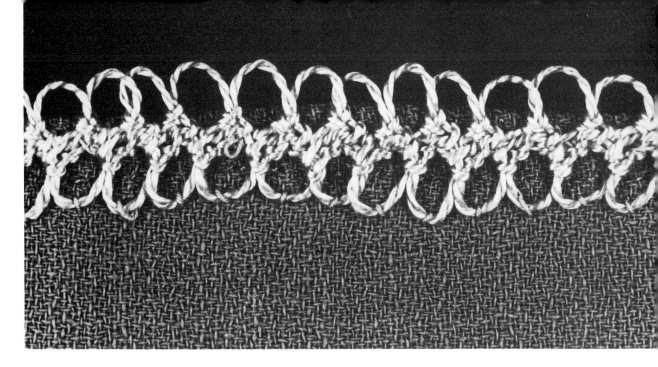

37 Perle cotton edging for a sleeve.

the work. Note that the number of loops means that both sides of the braid have the given number of loops.

Calculate as follows: multiply the number of loops per 2.5 cm (1 in) by the required length.

When finishing off leave a length of yarn so that more loops may be added if needed.

Working long lengths of braid

To avoid repeated counting of loops tie a marker thread to each fiftieth loop.

As the braid leaves the pin it is inclined to twist and may become distorted as the work grows. Rolling the braid up and tying it loosely with a piece of wool will keep it under control.

Applying the braids

For good results, it is important that the braids are applied with care. They should be stretched to the best effect with the loops equally distributed. Always use a matching thread for stitching down except where stitchery is part of a decorative scheme.

1 Pin the braid onto the fabric at each end. If the length is not satisfactory add or pull back the loops as required. Place a pin in the middle and then as many in between as needed. The loops should now be evenly distributed.

2 Use a matching thread to stitch down the middle crochet (now called the spine). Take a small stitch on the top side and a longer stitch underneath. The top stitch should be small enough to 'bed' into the crochet making it almost invisible.

3 Stitch down the tips of loops according to the type of braid:

38 A tea cosy with hairpin braid.

The decorative braid. The stitches should not be pulled too tight, try using a double thread for bold results.
The wool braid. Stitch down the loops on both sides.
The perle cotton braid. Stitch down the inner loops only.
4 Press lightly.

Projects using the basic braid

At this stage the main techniques of making a basic braid have been covered. This chapter finishes with two patterns for a tea cosy and a cushion cover. The hairpin braid is used as an adornment and much consideration has been given to its working and application. For a good result make the articles on which it is used with the same care and attention to detail. Use suitable fabrics as directed, press the fabric before starting, measure the pieces carefully on the straight, i.e. parallel to the selvedge, sew with matching thread and stitch the seams evenly to the given allowance. There are no complicated sewing processes and although the articles can be stitched up by hand a sewing machine will be more efficient.

The crochet instructions are set down in the customary manner using abbreviations. The making up instructions are fully explained.

Additional abbreviations are: (m) metre, (yd) yard.

A tea cosy   Measures 24 × 20 cm (9 × 8 in) (figure 38)

This cosy will fit a two cup teapot. It uses five lengths of braid set between double lines of quilting. The edge is finished with a rayon cord. A soft material should be used to show the quilting effectively, so choose from lightweight satin, tricel lining or poly

36

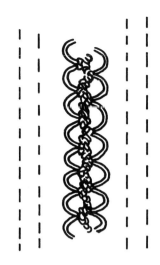

39 Detail of the tea cosy. (The dashes represent quilting lines.)

cotton. The cosy shown here is made entirely in pink but contrasting colours would be equally attractive. The quilting can be worked either by hand or machine. Figure 39 shows the braid and quilting in detail.

Materials
Two pieces of material 30 cm (12 in) square (⅓ m or yd). The same of lining which can be the same as the outer fabric.
Two pieces of interlining in muslin or very soft cotton, and of synthetic wadding all measuring as above. The wadding is obtainable at haberdashery or fabric shops.
¾ m (yd) of rayon cord. Matching thread.
For the braid, perle cotton No. 5, 15 mm (½ in) hairpin, 2.00 mm hook.

Method
1 Work the following lengths of braid to a tension of 4 loops per 2.5 cm (1 in) when stretched.
One centre braid – 38 loops, two middle braids – 36 loops, two outer braids – 32 loops.
2 Trace a pattern from figure 40. 1.5 cm (½ in) turnings are allowed. Cut out two pieces of all the materials listed.
3 For the front, using a soft pencil very lightly draw the broken and solid lines onto the right side of the face piece.
4 Pin and stitch the braids onto the broken lines.
5 Sandwich the wadding between the face piece and one piece of interlining. Tack all round the edge.
6 Tack between each pair of solid (quilting) lines. Stitch on the solid lines by machine or hand using small running stitches. Remove the tackings and trim the outside edge to reduce bulk.
7 For the back, tack the remaining wadding and interlining together round the outside edge and then tack in vertical lines about 5 cm (2 in) apart. This is permanent to hold the wadding in place.
8 Place the remaining outer piece on top of the wadding, tacking round the edge.
9 *To make up* pin and tack the completed front and back pieces with the right sides together. Stitch all round the curved edge. Turn up the lower edge 1.5 cm (½ in) and tack.
10 Turn to right side and stitch the cord around the curved edge. Fray out each end to reduce bulk, and secure.
11 For the lining. Tack the two pieces together 2.5 cm (1 in) from the curved edge and stitch close to the tacking. Trim the excess as the bulk of the quilting reduces the size.
12 Turn up and tack the bottom edge. Slip inside the cosy and slip stitch in place.

A cushion cover   Measures 41 cm sq (16 in sq) (figure 41)
The diagonal bands of basic braid are used here for a textured

40 The tea cosy pattern.

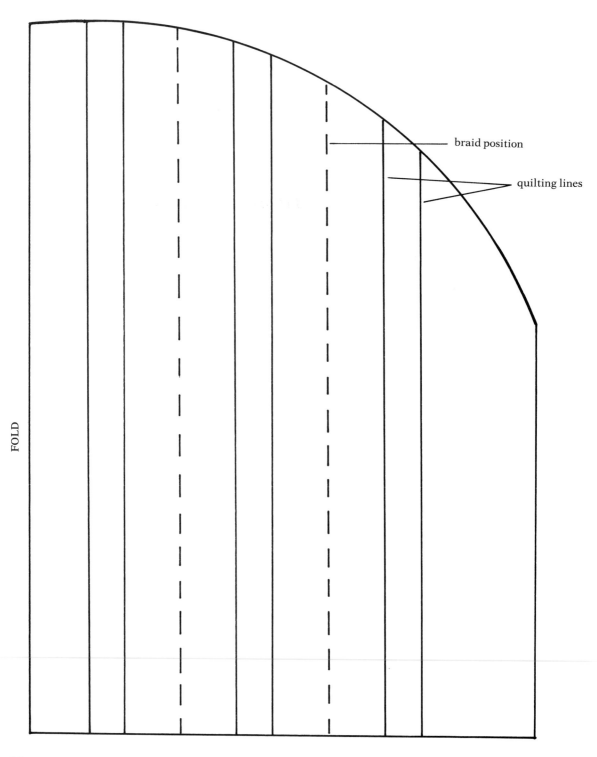

FOLD

braid position

quilting lines

41 A cushion with hairpin braid.

effect. Two widths of braid are used with two different yarns. A firm furnishing fabric is essential for a good texture as it will allow the braids to lie on the surface. The edge is finished with a crocheted cord and tasselled corners.

The cushion illustrated is made in a natural Aran shade but rich colours, especially in related shades, will give a very dramatic effect. Consider purple and deep pink on a crimson fabric, or turquoise and lime on dark green.

Materials

½ m (yd) of firm furnishing fabric to cut two pieces 41 cm sq (16 in sq).

For the braid, 50 g Aran type yarn, 25 mm hairpin, 4.50 mm hook.

25 g double knitting, 20 mm hairpin, 4.00 mm hook.

For the cord, Aran yarn and a 7.00 mm hook.

A cushion pad 41 cm sq (16 in sq).

Method

Figure 42 shows how the braids are arranged. The wide Aran braid is in the centre with the two narrower double knitting braids on either side.

1 *The Aran braids* are worked to a tension of 2 loops per 2.5 cm (1 in).

The central Aran braid is 56 cm (22 in) long, approx. 44 loops.

42 Detail of the cushion.

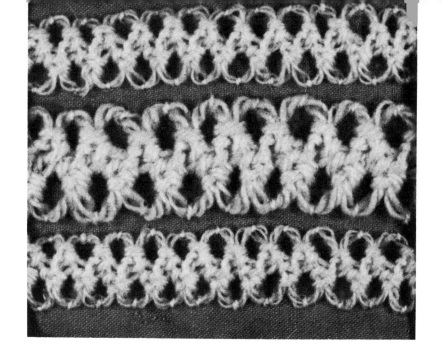

43 Cushion cover diagram.

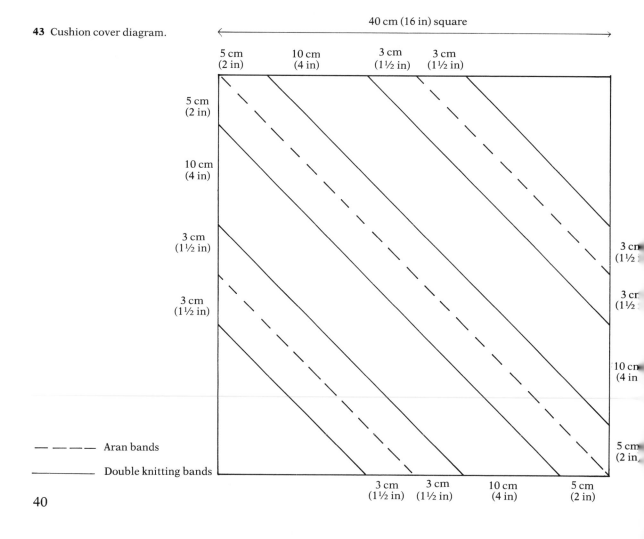

40 cm (16 in) square

5 cm (2 in) 10 cm (4 in) 3 cm (1½ in) 3 cm (1½ in)

5 cm (2 in)

10 cm (4 in)

3 cm (1½ in)

3 cm (1½ in)

3 cm (1½ in)

3 cm (1½ in)

10 cm (4 in)

5 cm (2 in)

— — — — Aran bands

———— Double knitting bands

3 cm (1½ in)   3 cm (1½ in)   10 cm (4 in)   5 cm (2 in)

44 Making a tassel:

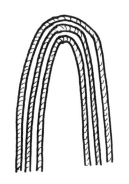

a) folding the yarn;

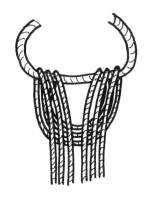

b) passing the folded end through the loop;

c) passing the cut ends through the fold.

The outer Aran braids are 31 cm (13 in) long, approx. 24 loops. *The double knitting braids* are worked to a tension of 3 loops per 2.5 cm (1 in).

The 2 central braids are 50 cm (20 in) long, approx. 60 loops.

The 2 inner braids are 37 cm (14 in) long, approx. 40 loops.

The 2 outer braids are 26 cm (10 in) long, approx. 24 loops.

2 Figure 43 gives the measurements for the braid lay-out. Make a full size paper pattern then use it to mark the braid positions on the right side of one piece of fabric. 1.5 cm (½ in) turnings have been allowed. Join the diagonal lines with pencil and ruler. The broken lines show the Aran braid position, the solid lines are the double knitting braid positions.

3 Working from the centre outwards, stitch the braids down with matching yarn. Place the spine of each braid exactly over each pencil line.

4 *To make up* stitch along the seam line on one side only of both the front and back pieces. These will form the cushion opening and will prevent the material stretching.

5 Place both pieces, right sides together, and stitch all round the three remaining sides curving the stitching round the corners. Trim away the excess material at the corners and any bulky braid ends. Overcast each opening edge separately, then continue round the other three sides. Turn the cover to the right side.

6 *To make the cord* use the Aran yarn double. With a 7.00 mm hook make a loose chain 1¾ m (2 yd) long. Now use a single Aran yarn with the 4.50 mm hook, turn and work 1 sl st loosely into each chain. Fasten off.

7 Place the chain side of the cord onto the cover seam and stitch firmly in place, twisting the cord to make small loops at the corners. Stitch just inside the stitching line of the front opening edge.

8 Place the pad into the cushion cover and turn in both opening edges on the stitching lines. Slip stitch firmly.

9 *To make the tassels* use five 20 cm (8 in) lengths of Aran yarn for each one. Knot into the corner twists as shown in figure 44: a) fold the yarn lengths double, b) pass the folded end through the corner twist, c) using the larger hook pull the cut ends through the folded end and tighten.

8 Headings

It is obvious that the basic braid is very versatile, and the worker will now feel ready to move on to finer work with crochet cottons. The braid can be made a little more elaborate by adding crocheting after the braid has been taken from the pin. This is done by crocheting into the loops using the double crochet, the chain, and occasionally the treble. The photographs in this chapter show the additional crochet (now called headings) in a contrasting colour so that it can be identified, but it also looks very attractive. When both the braid and the heading are worked in the same colour, the result looks quite intricate. A heading can also have a practical use in that sometimes the loops may twist when taken from the pin, especially when the tighter spun mercerised cottons are used. This chapter shows a variety of headings which are suitable for finer edgings and insertions.

Working into the loops

Use a 20 mm (¾ in) pin, a 1.50 mm crochet hook and No. 10 crochet cotton to make a practice length of basic braid having 20 loops. Finish off and remove from the pin. This is now called a foundation braid. Some of the loops may have twisted already and more will possibly do so during washing if this type of braid is used as an edging. By using a row of crochet, the loops can be anchored into either a straight or twisted formation. The double crochet is worked into the loop whilst the chain is used to bridge the gap between the loops.

Making straight loops

Before making the additional crochet take up the foundation braid and insert the hook into the first loop from the front as in normal crocheting (figure 45). If any loop has twisted the hook is still inserted from the front, but just under the twist, which will then be pulled straight when the double crochet is made.

1 To start, make a slip knot on the hook and hold the yarn in the usual manner. Take hold of the braid at the cast-on end and

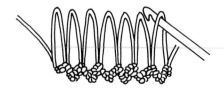

45 Inserting the hook into a straight loop.

42

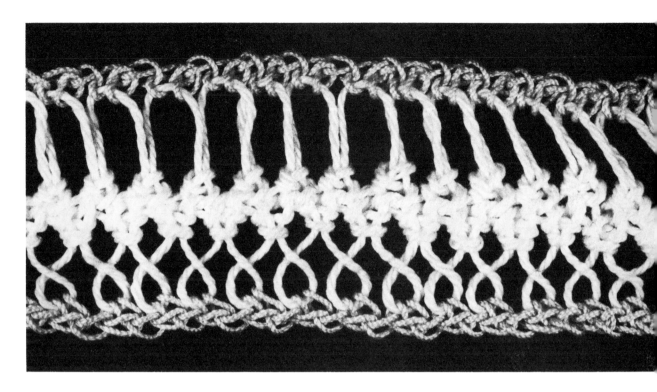

46 Braid with straight and twisted loops.

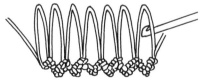

47 Inserting the hook for a twisted loop.

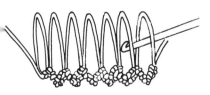

48 Picking up a group of loops.

carefully manipulate it so that the first loop is held between the thumb and first finger in the same position as the slip knot.

2 Insert the hook into the front of the loop to work 1 dc and 1 ch. Repeat to the end of the braid. The completed row is shown on the top side of figure 46.

Remember to move the fingers along the row to keep in control. In this instance, the double crochet should be worked firmly to hold the loop in position.

Making twisted loops

Again take up the hook, but this time insert it from the back of the loop (figure 47). When the double crochet is made from this position it will force the loops to twist. For loops that have already twisted, insert the hook into the tip of the loop. Work 1 dc and 1 ch into each loop as shown on the bottom side of figure 46.

Groups of loops (grp(s))

The top row on figure 49 shows an edging braid with pairs of twisted loops (called groups). With the hook, simply pick up two loops from the back (figure 48). The gap between the pairs of loops is now obviously wider, so this must be compensated by working sufficient chains to allow the loops to lie flat and even. Work on a practice braid as follows:

1 dc into a grp of 2 twisted lps, 3 ch. Repeat to the end. (See figure 49.)

43

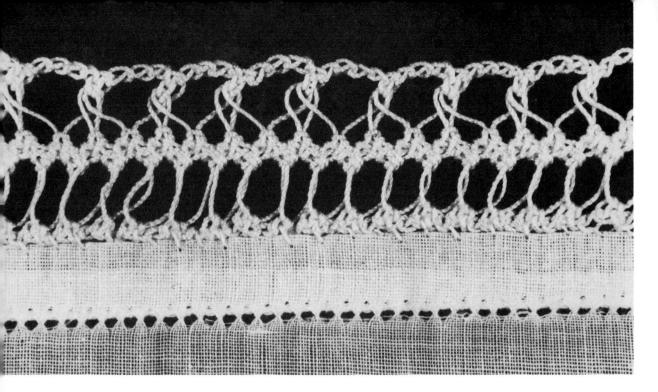

49 A pillow case edging.

Using the braid for full edgings

When using this type of braid as a full edging, a heading can be worked on one side only; the free loops are then sewn individually to the edge of the fabric. However, a heading does make a stronger edge for stitching, especially if the article is subject to wear. Figure 49 shows an edging with a plain heading worked as shown in figure 46 and now stitched on the fabric as a full edging. To apply the edging, place it onto the fabric with the edges together, pin as explained in Chapter 7. Oversew firmly but not too tightly, or the seam will not lie flat when opened out. Press.

Using a finer heading yarn

Most of the following patterns quote a finer cotton for the heading to avoid the actual braid being overwhelmed. The hairpin work is the prime attraction, any additional crochet should complement it.

When using a finer yarn than that used for the braid it will be almost always necessary to work more stitches than those needed on the practice pieces. The instructions allow for this and they also allow for a little stretch on the foundation braid as described in Chapter 7. Before embarking on the pattern it is wise to check the tension on a small practice piece to judge whether more or less loops are needed. If the subject of the pattern does not appeal, a small sample will provide valuable experience as they all contain a variation of the techniques used so far.

Reading the patterns

To avoid a clutter of repeated, basic instructions which apply to all the projects, note the following facts:

1 Always start the headings from the cast-on end of the foundation braid so that adjustments may be made to the length.

2 The crochet used for headings is mostly simple and obviously will be repeated to the end finishing with a double crochet.

3 When the heading is completed it will be finished off.

4 Before starting, study the relevant illustration to understand the working process.

A pillow case edging 2.5 cm (1 in) wide

Figures 46 and 49 make ideal edgings for bed linen. They are worked exactly as described for the practice pieces, but substitute No. 20 crochet cotton and a 1.25 crochet hook for the headings, and work two chains instead of one.

Tension – 6 lps per 2.5 cm (1 in).

Method

For a pillow case 48 cm (19 in) wide, work approx. 114 lps

For the first heading (figure 46).

Top side 1 dc, 2 ch into each straight lp ending with the dc.

Bottom side 1 dc, 2 ch into each twisted lp.

For the second heading (figure 49).

Top side 1 dc into a grp of 2 twisted lps, 4 ch.

Bottom side 1 dc, 2 ch into each straight lp.

A guest towel edging   2.5 cm (1 in) wide (figure 50)

The huckaback towel used here is 29 cm (11½ in) wide. The number of loops can be adjusted to any width but it must be an even number as they are taken up in pairs. The top heading has straight loops and an extra row of double crochet for strength. The bottom heading has groups of twisted loops into which three double crochet are worked to give a tiny shell effect. This last row used a contrasting pastel green (figure 51).

Materials

For the foundation braid, No. 10 crochet cotton, 20 mm hairpin, a 1.50 crochet hook.

For the headings, No. 20 crochet cotton, 1.25 hook.

Method

The tension is 6 lps per 2.5 cm (1 in).

1 Work a foundation braid of approx. 68 lps.

2 *Top heading* 1st row: 1 dc, 1 ch into each straight lp. Check the length at this stage. Turn with 1 ch.

50 A guest towel edging.

51 Detail of the towel edging.

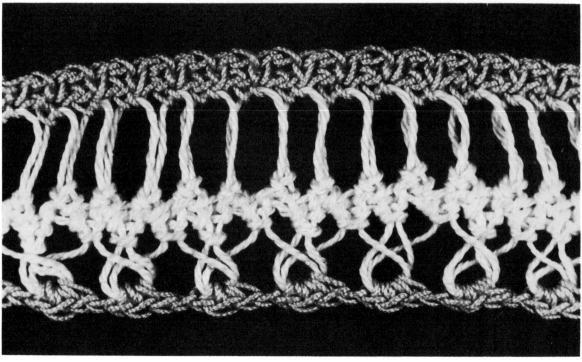

2nd row: 1 dc, 1 ch, into each dc of the 1st row.

3 *Bottom heading* 3 dc into each twisted grp of 2 lps, 1 ch. Oversew the edging in place.

A tray cloth insertion 40 × 28 cm (16 × 11 in) (figure 52)

Initially this tray cloth looks a little complicated but when taken one step at a time the worker will find that all the processes have been used before. The headings on the foundation braid are the same on both sides. The loops are taken up in groups of four, with four single loops between each group. There are two rows of heading, the first of double crochet and chains, the second of trebles, this being wide enough to cover the overcast edge of the cloth. The cloth is finished with a narrow crochet edging which echoes the bud shape of the four loop groups.

The instructions are set down in three sections – the tray cloth, the insertion, and the edging – each dealing fully with materials and method.

1 Materials for the cloth

One piece of suitable cotton or linen type fabric measuring 40 cm (16 in) × 32 cm (13 in) (turnings of 1.5 cm (¾ in) are allowed), or a purchased readymade cloth.

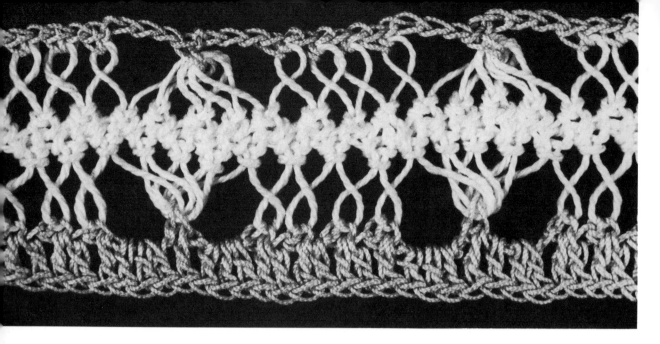

53 The insertion detail.

Method

1 Turn in all the edges ½ cm (¼ in) and press. Make a second turning of 1 cm (½ in). Press and hemstitch by hand or machine.

2 Mark a line 7 cm (2¾ in) from one end for the insertion. Make a line of running stitches ½ cm (¼ in) down each side of the pencil mark to prevent stretching. Cut along the pencil line and overcast by either machine or hand. In the latter case blanket stitch is the most suitable.

For readymade cloth, mark the cutting line and overcast as above.

2 Materials for the insertion

For the foundation braid, No. 10 crochet cotton, 20 mm (¾ in) hairpin, 1.50 crochet hook.

For the heading, No. 20 crochet cotton, 1.25 mm hook.

Method

Tension of 6 lps per 2.5 cm (1 in).

Make a foundation braid of 76 lps. Adjust this number if a different sized cloth is used.

Before starting work on the heading, study figure 53 which shows that all the loops are twisted and are taken up in sets of four. The top side shows the 1st row which clearly illustrates the four loop groups which are alternated with a set of 4 single loops. The braid starts and finishes with a set of 4 single loops.

Heading 1st row: 1 dc, 1 ch into 4 separate lps, 4 ch, 1 dc into a grp of 4 lps, 4 ch. Repeat from the beginning. 3 ch for turning ready for the second row.

Refer again to figure 53. The bottom side shows a row of trebles worked into the 1st row. Note that the trebles are worked into each stitch over the set of 4 single loops and into the space

A picot edging.

on either side of the group. Turn the book upside down to see how the row looks to the worker.

2nd row (1 tr into the 1st ch, 1 tr into the next dc) repeat twice more. These trebles, including the turning chain, should be standing on top of the block of 4 single loops. *3 tr into the next 4 ch space, 1 tr into the next dc (on top of the grp), 3 tr into the next 4 ch space (1 tr, into the next dc, 1 tr into the next ch). Repeat 3 more times.*
Repeat from * to * end.

Work the other side of the braid in the same way.

To make up place the inner edge of the heading exactly on the overcast edge of the cloth. Stitch down both inner and outer edges and press.

A picot edging (figure 54)

This is a simple but very useful edging, using only the chain and double crochet stitches. The edging illustrated used No. 10 crochet cotton and a 1.50 crochet hook.

Method
Work 4 ch, insert the hook into the 1st ch and make a dc, work another dc into the same place. *4 ch, 2 dc into the 4th ch from the hook* (i.e. the 1st ch of the 4 ch just made). Repeat for the desired length.

For the tray cloth, make the edging approx. 140 cm (55 in) long. This must allow for enough ease at the corners. Press.

Starting from the bottom left corner and from the cast-on end of the edging, oversew to the cloth taking it across the ends of the insertion. Press.

9 Narrow edgings for handkerchiefs

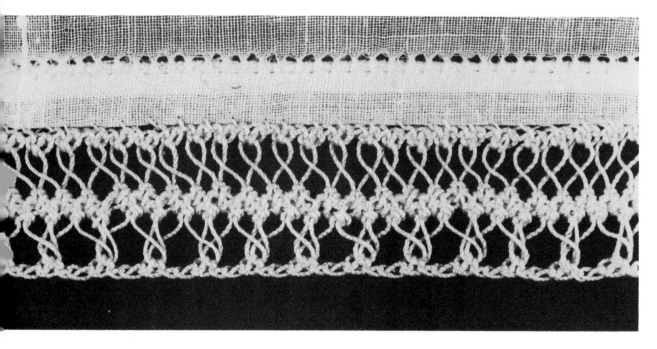

55 Handkerchief edging No. 1.

All the dainty edgings shown in this chapter are made on the narrowest hairpin available (10 mm) and use the fine No. 40 crochet cotton with a 1.00 mm hook. Edgings Nos. 1 and 2 are further variations of the headings shown in the last chapter with additional instructions for turning a corner.

Edging No. 1 (figure 55)

The loops on the inner edge are taken up singly whilst the outer heading takes the loops in groups of 2. The loops are twisted throughout.

Method
Tension – 9 lps per 2.5 cm (1 in)
1 Make a foundation braid long enough to go round a handker-

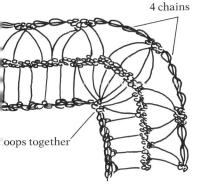

4 chains

loops together

56 Working the corner of No. 1.

chief using the tension as a guide and allowing 16 extra lps for the corners.

2 Work the inner heading first until it is long enough to fit along one side of the handkerchief making 1 dc into each lp.

3 For the corner take up 4 lps together with a firm dc (figure 56).

4 Count the number of lps on this first side, then work the remaining sides with the same number of lps.

5 Work the outer heading as follows: 1 dc into a grp of 2 lps, 2 ch. Repeat to the first corner. Lay the edging down flat to find the grp of lps which will come opposite the inner corner. Work 4 ch on each side of this corner grp (figure 56).

6 Oversew to the handkerchief and join the ends neatly. Press.

Edging No. 2 (figure 57)

The loops on both sides of this edging are taken up in groups of 2. The inner heading has a plain chain edge whilst the outer heading has an additional picot on the tips of the 2 loop groups. The loops are twisted throughout.

Method

Tension – 10 lps per 2.5 cm (1 in)

1 Make a foundation braid long enough to fit round a handkerchief allowing 16 extra lps for the corners.

57 Handkerchief edging No. 2.

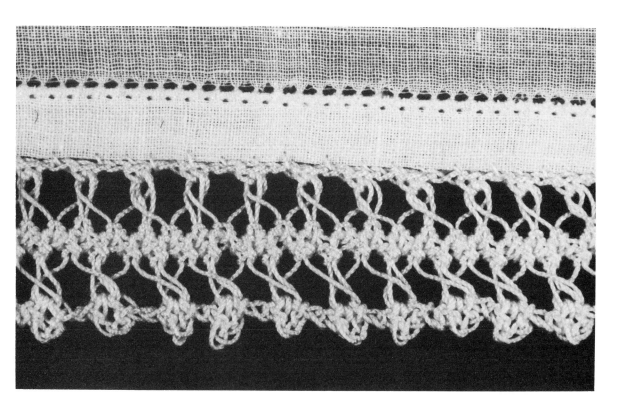

4 chains

4 loops together

58 Working the corner of edging No. 2.

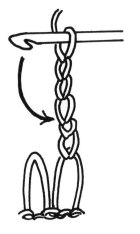

59 Making a picot.

2 Work the inner heading first until it is long enough to fit one side of the handkerchief.

1 dc into a grp of 2 lps, 2 ch. Repeat to the 1st corner.

3 Work the corner by taking up 4 lps together, 2 ch, (figure 58).

4 Count the lps on this side then work the 3 remaining sides in the same way.

5 To make a picot heading:

If the worker is not familiar with the working of a picot, practise first on a small foundation braid of 10 lps.

The heading and the picot are made in one operation. The picot is worked directly after the dc by working 3 ch and then making a sl st into the base of this ch which in effect is a tight ring (figure 59).

1 dc into the 1st 2 lp grp, 3 ch, sl st into the base of this ch (the picot is now complete), 2 ch. Repeat to the corner.

6 Lay the edging down flat to find the grp of lps which will come opposite the inner corner. Work 4 ch on either side of this grp (figure 58). Work the remaining sides in the same way.

7 Oversew to the handkerchief and join the ends. Press.

The following collection of headings are variations of the basic braid. The method of working remains the same, i.e. the pin is turned and the yarn is caught in the usual manner. The difference occurs at the double crochet stage where a variety of stitches are used. The loops are wider due to the additional

60 Handkerchief edging No. 3 using trebles.

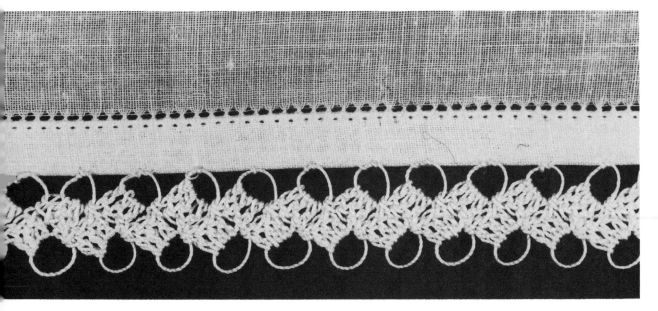

crochet so there is little danger of them twisting. The edgings are quickly made and are very interesting to work, a small sample of each one will certainly add to the expertise of the worker. They are ready for use when removed from the pin and will need only a slight stretch. Allow 8 extra loops for the corners. Advice on applying the wider loops is given after Edging No. 6.

Edging No. 3 (figure 60)

Tension – 3 lps per 2.5 cm (1 in).
Although this edging looks very different it is an easy variation in that the double crochet of the basic braid is replaced by 3 trebles. The pattern reads as follows:

3 tr into the front of the left loop, turn, 1 ch. Repeat as required.

Edging No. 4 (figure 61)

Tension – 5 lps per 2.5 cm (1 in).
This variation is worked as for the basic braid with the addition of 2 extra chains:

1 dc, into the left lp, turn, catch with 1 ch, then work 2 extra ch (3 in all). Repeat.

Edging No. 5 (figure 62)

Tension – 3 lps per 2.5 cm (1 in).
This version looks quite different. The double crochet is re-

61 Handkerchief edging No. 4 with extra chains.

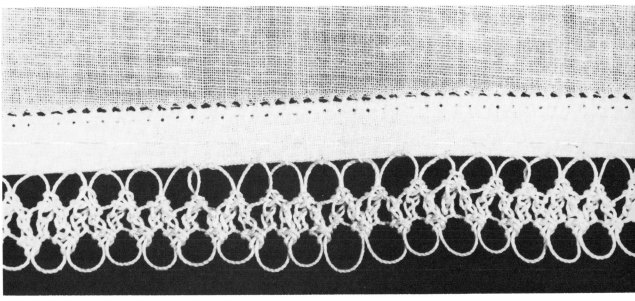

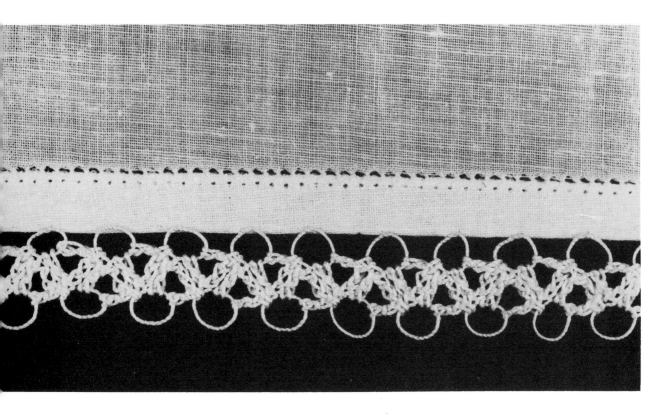

62 Handkerchief edging No. 5 with trebles and chain.

placed by 2 trebles and a chain making a triangular formation:
1 tr, 3 ch 1 tr all into the front of the left lp, turn, 1 ch. Repeat.

Edging No. 6 (figure 63)

Tension – 4 lps per 2.5 cm (1 in).
This dainty edging is a little more complicated, especially at the beginning, but extra care will be rewarding.

2 ch 1 dc into the front of the left lp, turn, *catch with 1 ch, 2 dc under the 2 ch of the previous round (at this stage the 2 ch will not be very distinct) 2 ch 1 dc into the front of the left loop, turn. Repeat from*. The 2 ch will now be easily seen.

Applying edgings with wide loops

Press the edging lightly with a slight stretch.
1 With the edging and handkerchief edges together pin down one side and count the loops.
2 Oversew by taking 2 or 3 tiny stitches into each loop, passing the needle invisibly through the hem to the next loop. Ease the edging round the corners by slightly drawing the loops together as they are stitched down.
3 Pin and stitch the other sides, having an equal number of loops on each. Press.

63 Handkerchief edging No. 6 with extra double crochet and chains.

Alternative edgings

All the edgings described in this and the previous chapter are interchangeable in that the wider braids shown in Chapter 8 can be made with the narrow hairpin, 10 mm (½ in) and fine cotton, whilst the edgings shown in this chapter may be worked in thicker yarn (perle cotton, Nos. 10 and 20 crochet cotton) with a wider pin, 20 mm (¾ in). Remember that the chosen yarn governs the size of the crochet hook, and that the width of the hairpin depends upon the desired width of the braid. If a thicker yarn, e.g. No. 10 crochet cotton, is used with the narrow pin, the central spine will almost fill the width of the prongs. The loops will then be much shorter, which may be ideal for certain purposes such as a decorative braid on clothes. Figure 36 shows this type of braid made with 4-ply wool, but this can be converted into a narrow, silky version using either mercerised crochet cotton, perle cotton, buttonhole twist or top stitching sewing thread such as Gütermann polyester. Braids made with sewing thread tend to twist, so each loop must be stitched down, but they are worth considering as the colour range for these is much wider than for crochet cottons. When converting the narrow edgings to a wider hairpin, make sure that the yarn is thick enough to avoid a spidery effect.

A table showing the size of crochet hook required for each type of yarn can be found in the introductory section to this book.

10 Curves and frills

It has already been noted that the basic braid has a fluent quality which allows it to form curves. Chapter 7 showed several ways of using a straight braid and Chapter 9 demonstrated the turning of corners, so by now the reader will be more aware of the braids' characteristics. For example a 20 mm (¾ in) wool type basic braid can form a curving band around a skirt hem, or a 15 mm (½ in) perle cotton braid can form simple initials (figure 64).

Stitching down curves

1 Draw the desired shape onto the fabric.
2 Pin the spine directly over the line and secure with small stitches.
3 Stitch down the loops allowing them to lie in their natural position.

A curved heading

A permanent curve is made by crocheting a close heading which will draw the loops together as shown in figure 65. To achieve this 1 dc is worked firmly into each loop of a foundation braid. When worked in a double knitting yarn on a 25 mm (1 in) hairpin it will make a charming edging for the neckline of a jumper. (Tension – 4 lps per 2.5 cm (1 in).)

64 A curved hairpin border with initial.

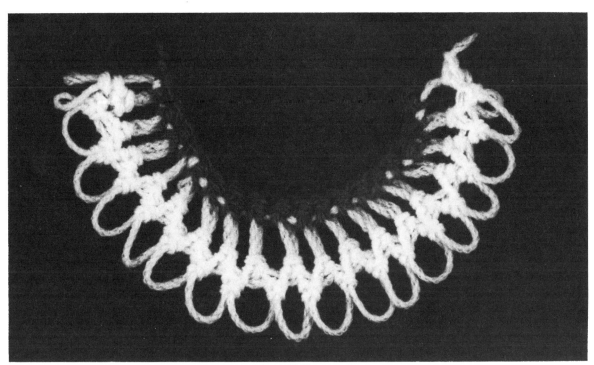

65 A curved heading.   **66** A hairpin braid frill.

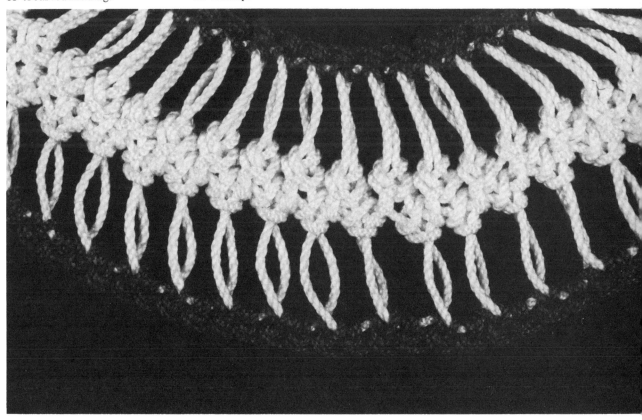

Making a frill

The bottom side of figure 65 shows how the loops have spread apart, so if a heading is worked on the lower side it must allow extra chains between the loops (figure 66). When the top edge is held at both ends and pulled straight the immediate result is a frill. The following pattern uses a frill edging of this type.

A frilled place mat   38 cm (15 in) × 31 cm (12 in) (figure 67)

This bright and attractive mat is made in a serviceable quilted material which is available from good fabric shops. The foundation braid is worked with a knitting and crochet cotton. The inner heading is also made with the same yarn whilst the outer heading uses a finer crochet cotton. The colours of the frill pick out the main colours of the floral design. Alternatively a ready made plain bound mat of this type may be found in some domestic linen or kitchen shops.

67 A place mat with a frilled edging.

68 Pattern for the place mat.

FOLD

FOLD

To make the mat

Each mat requires a piece of double sided quilting measuring 38 cm (15 in) × 31 cm (12 in).

1 Trace off a paper pattern from figure 68 which is one quarter of the mat. Fold a piece of paper into four and place the 2 straight edges of the pattern to the folded edges of the paper. Cut away the curved edge and open out.

2 Using the paper pattern cut out the fabric.

3 Finish the raw edge in one of the following ways: a) overcast by machine, b) blanket stitch by hand, c) bind with bias binding.

Making the frilled edging (figure 66 pulled straight)

Materials

For the foundation braid, 1 ball of Anchor knitting and crochet cotton No. 6 or Twilleys Lysbet (see list of mail order suppliers at the end of the book). 20 mm (¾ in) hairpin, 2.00 crochet hook. For the outer heading, No. 20 crochet cotton, 1.25 hook.

Method

Tension – 5 lps per 2.5 cm (1 in).

The loops are straight throughout.

1 Work a foundation braid of approx. 250 lps.

2 Work the inner heading, using the same yarn. 1 dc into each lp.

3 Work the outer heading with No. 20 cotton. 1 dc, 3 ch into each lp.

To make up

1 Join the ends of the edging together neatly.

2 Using the paper pattern as a guide, place a pin into the mat at each fold mark, thereby marking the edge into quarters.

3 Fold the edging into 4, also marking each fold with a pin.

4 Matching the pins place the edging around the edge of the mat having the outer edge of the spine just covering the edge of the fabric.

5 Stitch down the inner heading with small close hemming stitches.

A fine frill (figure 69)

This is a development of the place mat frill. The top heading remains the same to form the curve but the lower heading is a little more elaborate. Here the loops are twisted and also note that the chains between the loops are exaggerated by working one more chain than is necessary. When the edging is pulled straight these chains give an extra frilly effect. The finished frill is 2 cm (¾ in) deep and is made with No. 20 cotton which makes a lovely crisp collar edging for a special garment.

69 A fine frill.

Materials

For the foundation braid, No. 20 crochet cotton, 15 mm (½ in) hairpin, 1.25 crochet hook.
For the outer frill, No. 40 cotton, 1.00 hook.

Method

Tension – 10 lps per 2.5 cm (1 in).

1 Using No. 20 cotton, make a foundation braid the required length.

2 Using the same cotton, work the curved heading. 1 dc into each straight loop.

3 Using No. 40 cotton, work into the twisted lps. 1 dc, 4 ch into each loop. Finish off.

11 Hairpin motifs

The pliable quality of hairpin crochet is once again demonstrated in the making of motifs from short lengths of foundation braid. When the two ends are joined the loops on one side are gathered into the centre causing the outer loops to spread into a flower motif which can be used for many decorative purposes (figure 70).

Making a motif   6 cm (2½ in) diameter (bottom left on figure 70)

Assemble all the following items before starting the motif: Double knitting yarn, 25 mm (1 in) hairpin, 4.00 crochet hook, scissors. A blunt needle, either a bodkin or a tapestry needle threaded with matching cotton approx. 23 cm (9 in) long. This is

70 Four hairpin motifs.

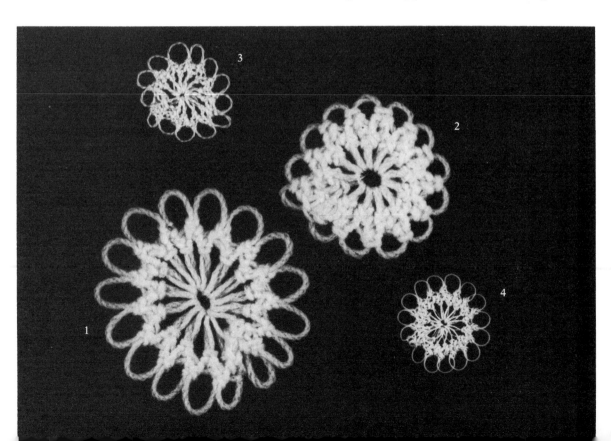

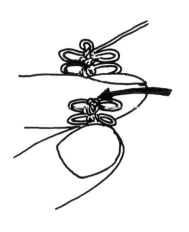

71 Joining a motif.

used for gathering the centre loops so avoid a silky thread as the ends must be knotted securely.

Method

1 Make a foundation braid having 16 loops but do not fasten off. Remove the hook from the last stitch which should be pulled longer to prevent it from pulling out. Cut the yarn leaving an end of approx. 8 cm (3 in).

2 Carefully remove the braid from the pin and wrap it round the first finger like a bandage. The 'cast on' end should be held between the thumb and first finger and the 'cast off' end between the first and second finger (figure 71).

3 Insert the hook into the spine at the 'cast on' end as arrowed then back into the stitch left at the 'cast off' end. Catch the yarn and draw it back to make a slip stitch so joining the two ends together. Do not make a tight slip stitch as this will distort the loops. Fasten off but keep the braid round the finger.

4 To gather the centre loops, which are those nearest the tip of the finger, and starting a few loops away from the join, run the gathering thread through the straight loops. Remove from the finger, draw up tightly and knot the ends securely, but do not trim the thread.

5 Open out the motif and run in the ends. The ends of the gathering thread are used to stitch down the centre of the motif. Press lightly.

Motif variations

Figure 70 shows three more versions of this motif which are all worked in the same manner but the yarns, hairpin widths and the number of loops are varied.

Motif 2   5 cm (2 in) diameter (top right on figure 70)

This motif is also made with double knitting yarn but it is worked on a narrower hairpin which results in smaller loops. Using a 20 mm (¾ in) hairpin work a foundation braid of 13 loops.

Motif 3   3 cm (1¼ in) diameter (top left on figure 70)

The two small motifs are made on the narrow hairpin. Use a 15 mm (½ in) hairpin, perle cotton No. 8, 1.75 crochet hook to make a foundation braid of 13 loops.

Motif 4   3 cm (1¼ in) diameter (bottom right on figure 70)

Use a 15 mm (½ in) hairpin, No. 20 crochet cotton, 1.25 crochet hook to make a foundation braid with 16 loops.

There are many ways of using these pretty motifs. The following ideas show two methods of enhancing a plain garment.

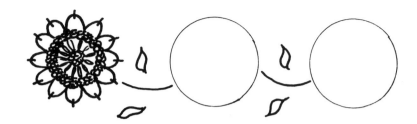

A daisy chain (figure 72)

Figure 72 features a row of motifs for a small girl's dress using the perle cotton motif numbered 3. The tips of the loops (petals) are stitched down with three strands of pink embroidery cotton, the eye of the daisy can be either a small yellow button or a bead stitched on very firmly. Stems and leaves can be added using stem stitch and lazy daisy.

Appliqué flowers on a waistcoat (figure 73)

A colourful medley of motifs stitched onto the back of a waistcoat is both cheap and quick to make. A mixture of yarns will give added interest provided they are all shrink resistant should the garment need frequent washing.

Method
1 Cut out several circles of paper to the same diameters as the motifs in figure 70. Arrange and pin them on the chosen background, using figure 73 as a guide.
2 Make the motifs and stitch down the centres with the gathering threads first, and then stitch the loops. Buttons and beads can also be used to great effect. Finish with embroidered stems.

  This type of design could also be used for a cushion cover.

A wheel motif (figure 74)

As shown in the illustration, this motif has a heading which is worked in the same way as the headings featured in Chapter 8. The number of chains between the loops is adjusted to ensure that the motif will lie flat. The largest motif on figure 70 is used as the base with the additional heading worked in a contrasting 4 ply yarn.

Making a wheel motif   7.5 cm (3 in) diameter
1 Make the large motif numbered 1 on figure 70.
2 For the heading use a matching 4 ply yarn, a 3.50 crochet hook and work as follows:

  1 dc into a lp, 3 ch. Repeat round the motif finishing with 3 ch. Sl st into the 1st dc. Finish off. Press.

73 Appliqué flower motif on a waistcoat.

74 A wheel motif.

3 Stitch down the centre, then the heading with hem stitch.
Figure 75 features the use of wheel motifs on a simple shopping bag. The motifs are made entirely in black for a dramatic impact. These can be stitched or glued in position with a fabric adhesive onto either a purchased or a home made bag.

A canvas shopping bag   40 × 33 cm (16 × 13 in)

Materials
½ m (½ yd) of canvas or hessian 90 cm (36 in) wide. 12 completed 7.5 cm (3 in) wheel motifs.

Method
1 Use the cutting plan (figure 76) as a guide. For the main part cut a piece of fabric 90 × 35 cm (36 × 14 in).
For the handles cut the remaining strip in two to give 2 pieces 45 × 10 cm (18 × 14 in).
2 Apply the motifs as shown in figure 76.
3 Fold the main piece across the middle on the fold line, right

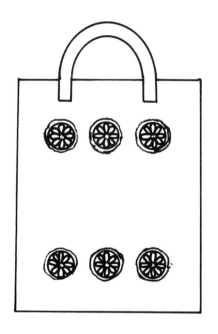

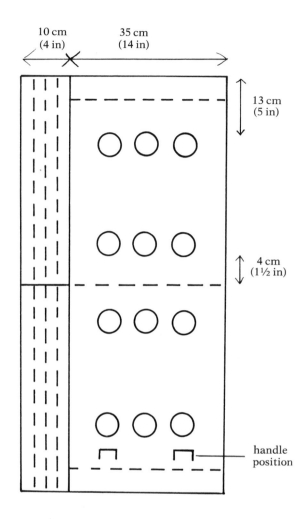

10 cm
(4 in)

35 cm
(14 in)

13 cm
(5 in)

4 cm
(1½ in)

handle
position

75 A shopping bag with wheel motifs.

76 Cutting plan for the shopping bag. (The dashes represent fold lines.)

sides together. Machine stitch down both sides and bind or overcast the raw edges.

4 Turn in the top edge 5 cm (2 in) and stitch.

5 To make the handles, turn in the long edges 2.5 cm (1 in) and press. Fold in half lengthways to give a 2.5 cm (1 in) wide strip. Press and stitch close to the edge.

6 Turn up the raw ends and stitch in place securely.

This plain bag would also look attractive with colourful bands of basic braid or the medley of flowers.

III

PRACTICAL WAYS WITH HAIRPIN CROCHET

12 For a baby

This collection of patterns uses the techniques learnt in Parts I and II. Some are very simple ideas using a novelty yarn. Ribbons and beads have been added to others. Some are quick and easy, big and bold, and others are fine and meticulous giving a real sense of achievement.

The patterns are set down in four categories and full working instructions are given with each one.

A curly bonnet edging (figure 77)

This easy method of making a pretty edging is perfect for babies' and children's knitwear. Two strands of baby wool are used together to make a basic braid: figure 78 shows one strand of white and one of blue.

Materials
2 small balls of baby wool, 25 mm (1 in) hairpin, 4.50 crochet hook. If the yarn is loosely spun it may be necessary to change the hook size to ensure that both strands will 'sit' in the hook.

Method
Tension – 3 lps per 2.5 cm (1 in).
1 Work a basic braid of approx. 40 lps. Fasten off and cut the wool leaving a long length for stitching down.
2 Pin the braid in place with the spine on the edge of the bonnet. Stitch the spine in place and allow the loops to go free.

77 A baby's bonnet edging.

A pram cover   50 × 45 cm (20 × 18 in) (figure 79)

Hairpin crochet braid and flower motifs are used to decorate this easy-care nylon quilt. The edging has a narrow ribbon threaded through the inner loops which matches the colour of the motifs. Synthetic materials and yarns are used throughout.

Materials for the quilt
1 piece of double-sided quilted fabric measuring 50 × 45 cm (20 × 18 in).

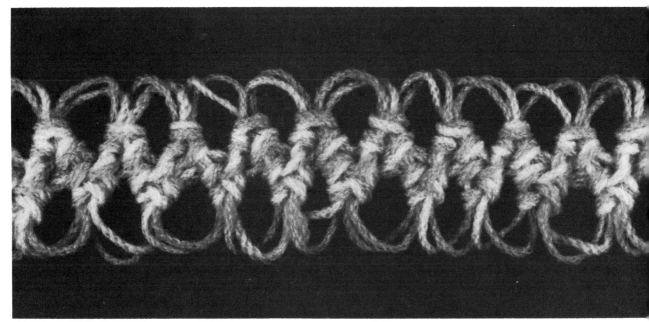

78 Detail of the bonnet edging using two colours.

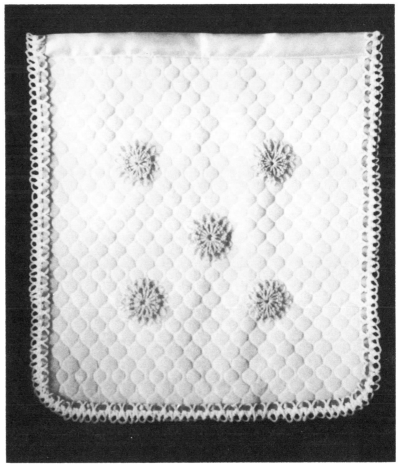

79 A pram cover with hairpin motifs and edging.

½ m (¾ yd) of matching blanket ribbon for the top edge.
1½ m (1¾ yd) of matching bias binding for the three remaining edges.

Method

1 To make the curve on the bottom corners, make a paper pattern first. On a square piece of paper measure and mark 2.5 cm (1 in) on either side of one corner and join with a curved line. Cut on the line and pin in position on the fabric and cut out both corners.

2 Bind the 2 sides and the bottom edge. Start at a top corner. Open out the binding and with the right side of the binding to the wrong side of the quilt, raw edges together, pin and stitch on the outer fold line of the binding.

3 Turn the binding over to the right side of the quilt and stitch on the fold line. The raw edge of the binding will be covered by the hairpin edging.

4 Bind the top edge. Measure the exact width of the top edge and add 2.5 cm (1 in). Cut the ribbon to this measurement, turn in 1.5 cm (½ in) at each end and press.

5 Pin and tack the ribbon over the top edge taking care to catch both sides of the ribbon. Stitch close to the edge. Slip stitch the 2 short ends of the ribbon.

Materials for the hairpin braids

25 g (1 oz) nylon double knitting yarn to match the quilt for the edging.
A small amount of contrasting double knitting yarn for the motifs.
25 mm (1 in) hairpin, 4.00 crochet hook.
1½ m (1¾ yd) narrow nylon ribbon 0.5 cm (¼ in) to match the motifs.

Method

1 Make 5 hairpin motifs having 16 lps. Apply to the quilt as shown in figure 79.

2 For the hairpin edging. Tension approx. 2½ lps per 2.5 cm (1 in). Make a braid with approx. 140 lps. The side edges will need about 50 lps, so check against the quilt and adjust if necessary. Tie a marker thread to the corner lp. The bottom edge will need about 40 lps, check again and mark in the same way. Make the 3rd side to match the 1st. Fasten off.

3 Thread the ribbon into the lps as shown in figure 80, keeping the ribbon flat.

4 Pin the spine to the edge of the quilt matching the marker threads to the bottom corners and ease the ribbon around the curves.

5 Turn under the raw edges of the ribbon and stitch firmly down the spine.

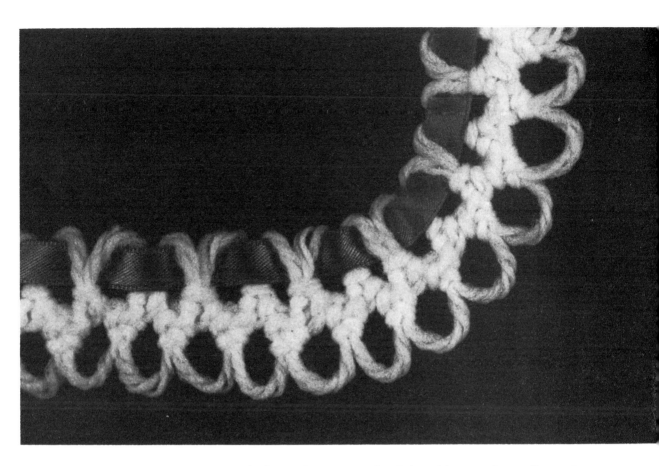

80 The pram cover edging with threaded ribbon.

6 Catch down the inner side of the ribbon with small matching stitches.

Variations

1 The curly two colour braid makes a good edging for a cot blanket. Use either a blanket fabric, a knitted blanket or a crocheted blanket. Here again refer to a crochet book to make a motif blanket or a straight patterned one.

2 A wide braid using two strands of 3-ply or 4-ply wool makes an eye-catching finish for a childs' winter coat, and on jumpers and jackets for any age group. Use a 35 mm (1½ in) hairpin and a 5.00 crochet hook. The hook size is approximate and depends on the type of wool.

3 A fine, ribbon-threaded edging for baby wear, e.g. round the hem of a dress, makes a dainty finish. Make up as for the pram quilt but use No. 20 crochet cotton, a 20 mm (¾ in) hairpin and a 1.25 crochet hook. Thread with very narrow contrasting baby ribbon.

$\underline{13}$ Just for fun

Here is a collection of novelties mostly using materials which are not usually associated with crochet. They do not take long to make nor is the cost too great.

A plant pot border (figure 81)

This quick and simple treatment for an ordinary plastic plant pot is ideal for fund raising events or as a small gift. Succulents and cacti look particularly attractive with this Mexican-type trimming made with parcel string.

Materials
7 cm (3 in) plastic plant pot (now available in a few colours).
Thin parcel string, 15 cm (½ in) hairpin, 3.00 crochet hook.
All purpose clear adhesive (e.g. UHU, Elmer's).

Method
Tension – 3 lps per 2.5 cm (1 in) when slightly stretched.
As string thicknesses may vary check the hook size before starting. Make a basic braid having approx. 25 lps. Fasten off. Stretch a little, apply the adhesive to the braid and stick in place. Trim the ends of the string.

This border can be adapted for larger pots. Matching saucers are also available in garden shops and can be given the same treatment if they are deep enough.

Alternatively the yarn could match the pot for a discreet embossed look, or use a toning colour for flowering plants.

A crayon pot (figure 82)

An empty tin or food container is converted into a bright crayon pot with the aid of felt and hairpin braid trimming on the top and bottom edges. Choose vivid, clashing colours that children love. This too is a cheap and easy gift especially when filled with pencils or painting sticks.

81 A plant pot border.

72

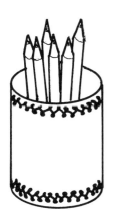

82 A crayon pot with decorative hairpin braids.

Materials

Straight-sided receptacle. (Paint the inside if desired.)
Felt piece to cover, adhesive.
4 ply yarn, 15 mm (½ in) hairpin, 3.50 crochet hook.

Method

Tension – 3 lps per 2.5 cm (1 in).
1 Measure the depth and circumference of the pot. Cut a piece of felt to size and check that the edges of the felt will meet but not overlap. Smear adhesive around the top and bottom edges and also where the felt edges will meet. Stick the felt down.
2 Make 2 lengths of basic braid calculating the number of lps from the given tension. Fasten off.
3 Stick down the braids and trim the yarn ends.

Or make a money box

If the container has a plastic lid the crayon pot can be converted into a money box by cutting a slot in the lid. This must be cut exactly in the centre so make a paper pattern by drawing around the lid. Cut the circle out, fold into four, make sharp creases and open out. Measure the slot 4 cm × 1 cm (1½ × ⅜ in) working from the centre crease and cut it out. Place this pattern onto the lid, mark the slot and cut using a craft knife. When taking measurements for the felt, keep the lid on and measure the depth from just under the lid.

A wooden bead choker   33 cm (13 in) (figure 83)

This choker, made from one length of basic braid, is ideal for casual wear or to add interest to a plain jumper. The beads are added during the working of the basic braid and the contrasting heading forms the curve. A little sparkle can be added by running a metallic thread through the heading. The choker is fastened at the back with a small button. The original was made with a beige braid, with a black heading through which shows a glint of bronze.

Materials

For the basic braid, Anchor knitting and sewing cotton No. 6, or Twilleys Lysbet, or a thin rayon parcel twine.
For the heading, perle cotton No. 5 with a short length of metallic yarn such as Twilleys Goldfingering, 12 wooden beads a little larger than a pea obtainable from craft shops or by post.
15 mm (½ in) hairpin, 2.00 crochet hook.
1 small button.

Method

Bead crochet. The correct number of beads are threaded onto the basic braid yarn before starting the crochet. They are then brought up and secured as given in the instructions. In this case

12 beads are added to alternate loops on one side of the front section.

1 Thread 12 beads onto the braid yarn. Cast on leaving a long end for stitching the button.

2 Work 19 lps of basic braid. Continue the braid bringing the beads up as follows. Turn, bring up one bead to lie close to the right hand prong, catch with 1 ch and 1 dc into the left loop as usual. Whilst working, the beads will slide inside the hairpin (figure 84) but when the hairpin is removed they will drop into the loop.

3 Bring the remaining beads up on each alternate lp on one side only.

4 Work 19 lps to match the first side. Finish off very tightly and remove from the hairpin.

5 For the heading, using the perle cotton, work 1 dc into each lp. If the metallic thread is used, hold it in the left hand so that it lies along the tops of the loops. It is then taken up with each loop when making the dc.

6 Finish off, run the ends in and stitch the button in place. Use the last hairpin loop for fastening over the button.

A lampshade   24 cm (9½ in) deep (figure 85)

Although figure 85 looks complicated it is made entirely of lengths of basic braid which are allowed to twist. They hang

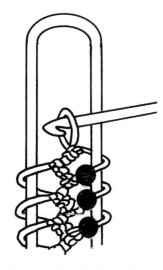

84 Working a hairpin braid with beads.

74

85 A lamp shade made with twisted hairpin braids.

from a lampshade ring, i.e. a wire ring with a small inner ring which fits onto the lamp holder. Each alternate braid has a bead threaded on the end which is held in place with a knot. The top edge is finished with a crochet chain cord. (For use with a 60 watt lamp.)

Materials
For the braid, 50 g (2 oz) of dishcloth cotton equivalent to Aran type yarn.
20 mm (¾ in) hairpin, 4.50 crochet hook, 7.00 hook for the top edging.
Lampshade ring 12 cm (4½ in) diameter.
Eight wood beads about the size of marbles. These should have holes which are just big enough to thread the yarn. Macramé beads have large holes and are not suitable.

All purpose clear adhesive.

Method

1 Make 8 basic braids with 20 lps and 8 with 18 lps finishing off as follows: when the correct number of lps are worked, carefully remove the hairpin keeping the crochet hook in position, then make 3 ch and finish off leaving ends of 5 cm (2 in).

2 The 2 lengths of braid are arranged alternately round the ring, with the twists all facing the same way. Fasten them in position by doubling the cast-on end over the ring and secure with either a stitch or adhesive.

3 For the top edging cord use 2 strands of the dishcloth cotton and with the 7.00 crochet hook make a chain to fit round the ring. Finish off and press flat. Apply the adhesive to the chain side of the cord and stick in position.

4 Thread the beads onto the 20 lp braids and make a knot to hold them. Knot the ends of the 18 lp braids just below the 3 ch. Finally, trim all the ends just below the knots.

For a party lampshade substitute the dishcloth cotton with Raffene. This is a shiny artificial raffia obtainable from craft shops. It comes in bright colours and would certainly add sparkle when lit.

A mobile   30 cm (12 in) deep (figure 86)

The lampshade can be adapted to make a mobile by the addition of six 26 loop lengths of braid fastened to the central light fitment. Coloured dishcloth cotton or any other firm yarn could be used for a young child's bedroom. Thread with bright beads or small bells but make sure these will not be too heavy.

To hang the mobile, measure 4 strands of yarn 30 cm (12 in) long. Tie these to the ring between each group of 4 braids before fixing the crochet cord in place. Gather the ends of the 4 strands together and tie onto a curtain ring for hanging.

Further suggestions

Useful for stocking fillers, small gifts and bazaars, the following ideas need only small oddments of wool in bright colours, pieces of felt and fabric. As a general guide use a 20 mm (¾ in) hairpin with double knitting or 4 ply wool. The braid can be stuck down with all purpose or fabric adhesive, or stitched down with a contrasting yarn as shown in Chapter 7.

To make a pencil case

Use two lengths of braid 18 cm (7 in) long, one piece of felt 18 cm sq (7 in sq), one 18 cm (7 in) zip matching either the felt or the braid.

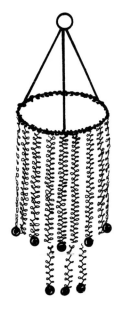

86 A hairpin braid mobile.

Method

1 Fold the felt in half, position and secure one length of braid on each side.

2 Turn inside out and stitch along the two short ends.

3 Open the zip and stitch in place. Turn the case right side out.

4 Make a small tassel for the zip as for the cushion cover in Chapter 7.

To make a comb case

Use two lengths of braid 15 cm (6 in) long, two pieces of felt 18 × 5 cm (7 × 2 in).

Method

1 Secure the braids in place on each piece of felt leaving 1.5 cm (½ in) at each end. Thread the ends through to the wrong side and stick down.

2 With the wrong sides together stitch round three sides 1.5 cm (½ in) from the edges.

3 Cut round the edges with pinking shears, if you have a pair.

A drawstring pump bag

One or more lengths of basic braid 50 cm (20 in) long. One piece of fabric 50 × 30 cm (20 × 12 in). One length of cord to match the braid 60 cm (24 in) long. A wider braid 2.5 cm (1 in) will look more impressive on a larger article, or use lengths of bright ribbon along each side of the braid. The hairpin braid could also be applied to a wider ribbon before being stitched to the bag.

Method

1 Stitch down the braid/s approx. 8 cm (3 in) from the bottom edge of the fabric.

2 With right sides together fold the bag in half. Stitch along the bottom and up the side.

3 For the drawstring channel, fold over 4 cm (1½ in) from the top edge. Turn the raw edge under and stitch leaving an opening for the drawstring.

4 Thread the cord through the channel and knot the ends together.

As hairpin braid is so pliable it is possible to form the child's initials, which could be added above the braid. Plan the positions of the braid and initials before stitching down.

For an apron

A broad band built up of braid and ribbon would make a pleasing decoration for a plain apron.

14 A Christmas miscellany

87 Hairpin braids on Christmas baubles.

Here is an opportunity to add an individual touch to Christmas. Hairpin braids are used for tree decorations, greetings cards and parcels using all the glitter and sparkle the festive season offers.

Christmas tree baubles (figure 87)

Plain medium size baubles are used for this attractive trio. Quickly made basic braids are glued in place.

Materials
Perle cotton No. 8.
15 mm (½ in) and 20 mm (¾ in) hairpins, 1.75 crochet hook.
Clear all purpose adhesive. Test a small amount on a bauble as some adhesives melt plastics.

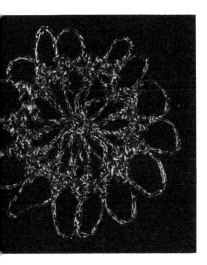

88 A silver star motif.

Method for the hairpin collar (left on figure 87)

1 Use the 20 mm (¾ in) hairpin to work approx. 21 lps, fasten off.

2 Using matching thread, gather the lps along one side so that it will fit round the neck of the bauble.

Method for the motif (centre on figure 87)

Use a 15 mm (½ in) hairpin to make 13 lps. Join and gather as explained in Chapter 2.

Method for the middle band (right on figure 87)

Use a 15 mm (½ in) hairpin to make approx. 36 lps. (The edgings in Chapter 9, figures 60–63 could also be used.)

To glue down, support the baubles in an egg box. Apply adhesives to the braids and stick in place butting the ends together. Other embellishments such as sequins and bows can be added by the adventurous worker.

A silver star motif   5 cm (2 in) diameter (figure 88)

A hairpin motif made with silver yarn immediately takes on the guise of a star when hung amongst the dark greenery of the Christmas tree. It is made with Twilleys Goldfingering – a metallic crochet yarn equivalent to 4 ply, available in a range of colours, the most popular being gold, silver and bronze. It is made on a 2.5 cm (1 in) hairpin which makes fairly long loops, some of which may twist, but for this purpose this seems to add to their attraction.

Method

1 With a 25 mm (1 in) hairpin and a 3.50 hook, make a basic braid with 15 lps and fasten off.

2 Gather the loops on one side with a matching sewing cotton and knot securely.

3 Open out the motif, glue the ends together and trim all the long ends.

4 Tie a fine thread to a lp for hanging.

This motif can be used effectively on party clothes, in which case follow the instructions in Chapter 11.

Christmas cards (figures 89 and 90)

Hand made Christmas cards are a pleasure to receive. The following suggestions do not take much time or expense and also give pleasure in the making. The first consideration is to find suitable blank cards which can be found in some artist supply shops. If these are not available, special stationery can be used: look for small pads of deckle edged writing paper in pale tints which, when folded, make a good shape. Heavy quality

89 A Christmas card with a gold motif.

90 A Christmas card with a hairpin holly wreath.

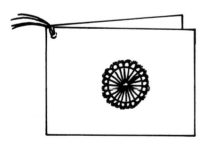

91 A gift tag.

note paper and matching envelopes in a bright range of strong colours are now stocked in some stationers and gift shops. When adorned with a simple sparkling hairpin motif, they are very effective. When folding these writing papers make sure to match the edges exactly and run a thumb nail down the fold to make a good crease.

Figure 89   4 cm (1½ in) diameter
Twilleys Goldfingering is ideal for this simple motif on a red paper. Using a 20 mm (¾ in) hairpin and a 3.50 crochet hook work 15 lps and finish off as instructed for the silver star figure 88. Before sticking to the card consider which will be the most attractive position. It does not have to be in the centre, this will depend on the size and shape of the card.

Figure 90   5 cm (2 in) diameter
A pale green deckle edged writing paper makes a background for this Christmas wreath made from a perle cotton basic braid. Red glitter on the spine represents shiny holly berries and a bow gives the finishing touch. Obviously this card is more time-consuming but worth the effort.

Materials
Green perle cotton No. 8, red glitter powder, narrow red craft ribbon or Raffene.
15 mm (½ in) hairpin, 1.75 crochet hook.
All purpose clear adhesive.

Method
1 Make a basic braid of 36 lps. Finish off.
2 Draw a circle 4 cm (1½ in) diam. on the card which should be just above half way up. Apply adhesive on this line which is the position of the spine.
3 Mark the 18th lp and, starting at the top of the circle, stick down both sides to meet at the bottom.
4 Run a thread of adhesive around the spine, sprinkle with glitter and allow to dry. Shake off the surplus glitter onto a paper. Tie a handsome bow and stick down.

Gift tags (figure 91)
These are made in a similar manner using a small motif.
1 Cut the cards 13 × 4 cm (5 × 2 in) and fold.
2 Using a perle cotton No. 8, 15 mm (½ in) hairpin and 1.75 hook, make a motif of 13 lps.
3 Stick the motif in place and add a sequin in the centre if desired.
4 Punch a hole in the top right hand corner and tie on a 12 cm (5 in) length of the perle cotton. Fold the cotton in half, thread

the double end through the hole, pass the 2 ends through the loop and tighten.

Cards and gift tags need not be confined to Christmas. Notelets made from a writing pad with a small hairpin motif make a nice gift.

A parcel rosette   7 cm (3 in) diameter (figure 92)

This crisp rosette is made with Raffene. Its shiny colourful qualities are perfect for tying up parcels and the addition of a matching rosette adds the finishing touch. When working with stiffer 'yarn' do not hook it onto the little finger of the left hand as for the normal crochet yarns. Hold it as shown in figure 4 (page 18) having the fingers close allowing it to slide through.

A very narrow knitting ribbon can be used, although this is not easily obtained. (Some haberdashery shops do stock it.)

Method
1 Use a 25 mm (1 in) hairpin and a 4.00 crochet hook to make a basic braid with 12 lps. Finish off.
2 Gather one side with matching thread and knot securely.
3 Glue the ends together and trim. Glue onto the parcel.

Raffene motifs could also be made as the sole decoration on a sophisticated Christmas tree. Make sufficient motifs and stick down a brilliant in the centre of each. Add glitter as described for the Christmas card shown in Figure 90.

92 A parcel rosette.

15 A Victorian collection

This book has so far used hairpin crochet for modern day requirements, but it is not quite complete without a look at the type of work our Victorian forebears produced. It was an age of excess embellishment, often to a state we would now consider of vulgarity, but even so the fine and intricate work deserves our admiration. Examples of Victorian needlework in museums often seem faded and limp due, of course, to the passage of time. These final patterns, perhaps a little frivolous, are based on the Victorian passion for fine lace, frills, and pretty pastel colours. They look as fresh and charming as Grandmother's work, most certainly, once was.

93 A beaded jug cover.

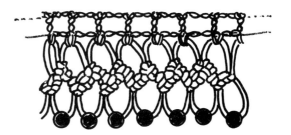

A jug cover (figure 93)

This is a very practical piece of Victoriana which is just as useful today. The centre is made from fine net or muslin and the deep edging of hairpin braid has a small bead held in each loop which act as weights to prevent the cover falling off. The beads are first threaded onto the crochet cotton and are secured in the loops as the basic hairpin braid is worked. This process is fully explained in the instructions. The top edge of the braid has a treble heading which conceals the raw edge of the net. The cover is efficient, decorative and hygienic since it is easily washed and put over a jug to dry. Figure 94 shows the detail of the edging.

Materials

For the centre, a 13 cm (5 in) round of fine curtain net or muslin (see the addresses at the end of the book).
For the basic braid, No. 10 crochet cotton, 20 mm (¾ in) hairpin, 1.50 crochet hook.
For the heading, No. 20 crochet cotton, 1.25 crochet hook.
56 small beads no more than 5 mm (¼ in) diameter with a hole large enough to take No. 10 crochet cotton. Old necklaces are a good source of supply.

Method

1 Cut out the fabric 13 cm (5 in) diam. With matching cotton make running stitches all round, 5 mm (¼ in) from the edge. This can be done by either hand or machine, allow the stitching to gather slightly.
2 Turn in the edge 1 cm (½ in) and with small stitches tack on the previous stitching. Trim away 5 mm (¼ in) from the raw edge very close to the stitching.
3 *Bead crochet.* Sit at a table when working with beads so that the weight is supported. Thread all the beads onto the No. 10 crochet cotton. One bead is brought up for each lp on 1 side only.
4 Cast on in the usual manner. Turn and insert the hook back into the stitch. Before working the ch st bring up 1 bead to lie close to the pin. Now work 1 ch, 1 dc as normal. Continue working the basic braid and bringing up a bead on one side only. The beads will lie on the inner side of the prong as shown on

figure 84. When working with small beads it may be more efficient to bring up several beads to hold in the left hand before hooking the yarn round the little finger. When all the beads are taken up end with 1 plain lp. Cut the end approx. 10 cm (4 in) long, finish off loosely and remove from the hairpin.

5 Work the heading with No. 20 cotton as follows:

   1st row: 1 dc, 2 ch, into each lp, 3 ch, turn.

   2nd row: 1 tr, 1 ch, into each dc of the previous row.

Note that the 2nd row of the heading is drawn in a little to accommodate the curve of the fabric. Finish off loosely as for the braid.

6 Stretch the braid to 4 lps per 2.5 cm (1 in). Press lightly.

7 Join together the ends of the braid and heading by unpicking the loose finishing off stitches. Insert the hook and join with a sl st and finish off.

8 To make up, fold the centre piece into 4 and mark each fold with a pin. Fold and mark the edging in the same way. With the raw edge of the centre piece uppermost, place the edging onto the fabric matching the pins. Have the dc row of the heading exactly on the edge, the tr row should then just cover the raw edge as on figure 94.

9 Stitch down both rows of the heading very firmly. Run in all loose ends.

A pin cushion   9 cm (3½ in) diameter (figure 95)

A large hairpin motif with three rows of heading incorporating small pearls is stretched over a round pad. The motif has a slight variation of the basic braid in that 2 double crochets are worked into the left loop instead of one. The first round of the heading forms the twisted loops, the second round takes up the pearls which are held between two chain stitches and the final round makes a shell edging with groups of trebles. Although this is a frivolity, it is interesting to make.

Materials

For the pad, 2 pieces of soft satin or tricel lining 10 cm (4 in) square. A small amount of kapok or soft toy filling.

For the motif, No. 10 crochet cotton, 35 mm (1½ in) hairpin, 1.50 crochet hook.

For the heading, No. 8 perle cotton to match the pad, 1.75 hook. 12 small pearl beads, 1 larger bead for the centre.

Method

1 To make the pin cushion cut out 2 rounds of fabric 10 cm (4 in) diam. With a seam allowance of 1.5 cm (½ in) stitch round the edge, leaving an opening for stuffing. Trim the seam allowance to remove the bulk. Turn to the right side and stuff well to make a plump pad. Slip stitch the opening edges together.

95 A pin cushion.

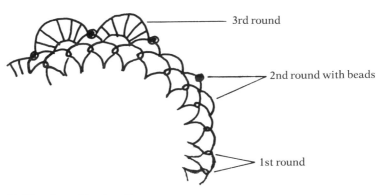

3rd round

2nd round with beads

1st round

96 The pin cushion heading.

2 To make the motif. Work as for the basic braid motif but work 2 dc instead of 1 into the left lp. Work 24 lps, join the ends, gather the centre as shown in Chapter 11.

3 Work the heading using the perle cotton. Thread on 12 pearl beads which will be used on the 2nd round. Figure 96 shows how the 3 rounds of the heading are built up.

    1st round: 1 dc into 1 twisted lp, 3 ch. Repeat all round the motif. Join to the 1st dc with a sl st.

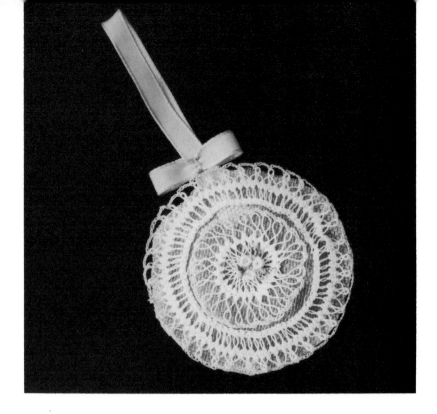

2nd round: 1 ch, *1 dc into the 2nd ch of the 1st round, 3 ch, 1 dc into the next 2nd ch, 2 ch, bring up a bead to lie next to the hook, 2 ch.* Repeat from * to * all round. After the last 2 ch, sl st into the 1st ch of the round. Fasten off.

3rd round: using No. 10 crochet cotton, make a slip knot on the hook. Work 1 dc into the 2 ch space on the left side of a bead. *Work 5 trs into the next 3 ch space, 1 dc into each side of the next bead, keeping the bead in front. Continue from * all round then 1 dc into the right side of the 1st bead, sl st into the 1st dc and fasten off.

4 To make up stretch the motif over the pad and, working at the back, pin and stitch the 1st heading row to the edge of the pad. Run in all the ends. Stitch the larger pearl in the centre of the motif.

A pomander 8 cm (3 in) diameter (figure 97)

Frilly herb sachets are the very essence of the Victorian and Edwardian era. They were an essential element in a lady's wardrobe because the clothes of that time were not laundered as regularly as today. In fact some gowns were so elaborate that washing was impossible so pomanders were used to keep them fragrant. Herbal sachets have been used for hundreds of years to mask the more unpleasant odours, but those made by the ladies of the last century were probably more decorative than at any other time.

    This pomander is made with a double layer of net and filled

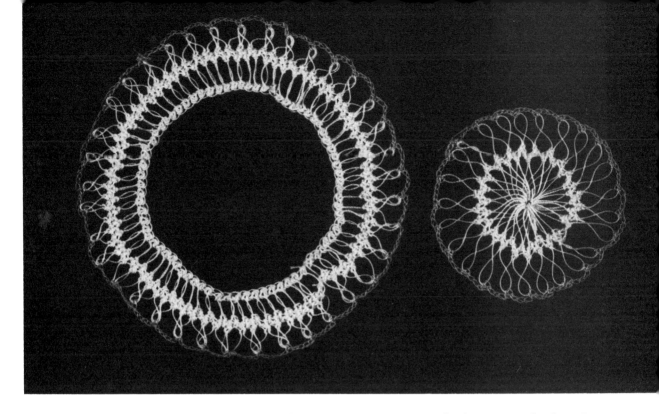

98 The motif and edging for the pomander.

with either lavender or pot pourri which can now be found in gift shops and larger chemists. Fine hairpin crochet is used on the front, consisting of a central motif and a curved edging (figure 98). A ribbon for hanging and a tiny nosegay in the centre add the finishing touch. Made in pastel colours of blue, pink and white – lovely for a bridal trousseau.

Materials

For the sachet, 4 pieces of pink dress or window net 10 cm (4 in) square. 30 cm (12 in) of pale blue narrow ribbon.

Lavender or pot pourri, 1 small pearl button. Tiny flowers as used on lingerie from haberdashery shops or artificial forget-me-nots.

For the motif, No. 40 white crochet cotton, 20 mm (¾ in) hairpin, 1.00 crochet hook.

For the edging, as for the motif but use a 15 mm (½ in) hairpin. For the headings, No. 60 pale blue crochet cotton, 0.75 crochet hook.

Method

1 To make the sachet. On 1 piece of net draw a circle 6.5 cm (2½ in) diam. Pin all 4 pieces of net together and stitch on the pencil line through all the layers, leaving a 2.5 cm (1 in) opening for the filling.

2 Fill with the chosen herbs. Cut a 20 cm (8 in) length of ribbon, fold in half and insert into the opening. Stitch across the opening, making sure the ribbon is secure.

3 Cut away the excess net 5 mm (¼ in) outside the stitching line.

4 To make the motif. Using No. 40 cotton and a 20 mm (¾ in) hairpin, work a basic braid with 30 lps, join and gather the centre as shown in Chapter 11.

5 For the heading, use No. 60 cotton and work as follows:

1 dc, 4 ch into each twisted lp. Repeat all round and join to the 1st dc with a sl st. Fasten off.

6 To make the edging, use No. 40 cotton and a 15 mm (½ in) hairpin. Work a basic braid of 78 lps, fasten off loosely.

7 For the inner heading, use No. 40 cotton.

1 dc into each lp all round, join to 1st dc with a sl st. Fasten off.

8 Undo the end of the basic braid to join the ends of the spine with a sl st. Fasten off.

9 For the outer heading, use No. 60 cotton.

1 dc into a grp of 2 twisted lps, 5 ch, all round. Join to the 1st dc with a sl st, fasten off.

10 To make up. Place the motif in the centre of the sachet and with the button on the reverse side stitch through the button and the sachet drawing up tight. Stitch the inner heading of the edging in place. Make a bow with the remaining length of ribbon by folding it in half, with the raw edges at centre back, and secure with a few stitches. Glue the flowers in the centre.

Using a Victorian hairpin (figure 99)

Figure 99 shows an old hairpin with finer prongs than those obtainable today. It makes very dainty loops when working with the finer crochet cottons, i.e. Nos. 40, 60 and 80. This type of pin can sometimes be found in the work boxes of the older generation, or they can be made. Fine steel knitting pins with points at both ends are ideal as they can be heated slightly and bent to the width shown in the full size illustration. Most modern hairpins sold for hairdressing are too flimsy and will give uneven results, but it may be worthwhile experimenting. Take care that the prongs are not drawn together whilst working. Any of the edgings in Chapter 9 can be used with this type of pin. No. 60 crochet cotton with a 0.75 crochet hook is recommended for delicate work, an example of which is shown in the following final pattern.

99 A fine Victorian hairpin.

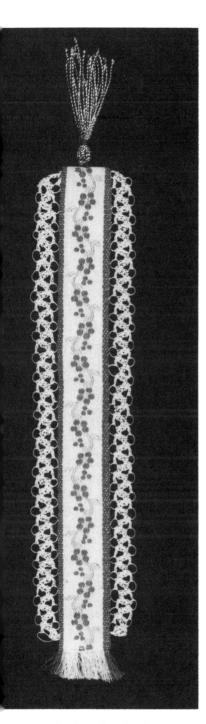

100 A bookmark with a fine hairpin edging.

A bookmark (figure 100)

A pretty bookmark made with a narrow floral ribbon edged with delicate hairpin crochet will surely add to the pleasure of reading. The ribbon is used double and is therefore reversible; a matching tassel completes the picture. Edging No. 5 (figure 62 on page 54) was chosen for the bookmark illustrated here, but any of the edgings Nos. 3–6 are equally suitable.

Materials

38 cm (15 in) of ribbon approx. 20 mm (¾ in) wide.
For the edging, No. 60 crochet cotton, a fine hairpin (10 mm if a finer one is not available), 0.75 crochet hook.
For the tassel, a matching yarn either No. 20 crochet cotton or perle cotton No. 8.

Method

1 Work 2 lengths of hairpin edging 22 cm (8½ in) long, approx. 26 lps. Finish off and press lightly.
2 To make the tassel cut ten 10 cm (4 in) lengths of the tassel yarn. Use a length of the same yarn to tie the strands together in the middle leaving the long ends for joining to the ribbon. Fold the bundle of strands in half and wind a thread just below the top, finishing with a knot. Trim the ends of the tassel to equal length.
3 To make up, fold the ribbon in half. Thread the long ends of the tassel into a needle, one at a time, and pass them through the fold of the ribbon to the inside. Knot together and trim.
4 Tack the folded ribbon down the centre, then stitch the edgings in place as shown in figure 100 making sure to catch both edges of the ribbon.
5 Fray the bottom end about 1 cm (⅜ in).

A variation

A bookmark made in the same way but using a plain satin ribbon will make a very personal gift if the recipient's initial is worked onto the ribbon. The width of the ribbon will only allow for a small letter, so a couched thread will be more successful unless the worker has some embroidery skill. A metallic couched thread will make the bookmark extra special.

To couch a letter

1 Draw the outline of the folded ribbon on paper. Draw in the letter in a satisfactory size and position.
2 Copy this onto the ribbon with a faint pencil line.
3 Thread the couching thread into a needle, bringing it through the ribbon from the wrong side at the starting point of the letter. Follow the letter round and take it through to the wrong side at the finishing point. Some letters will need more than one thread,

e.g. 'A' will start at the left base, up to the apex and down the second leg. Couch down this outline first, then add the crossbar in the same manner.

4 Use a fine matching sewing thread and catch down the couching thread with tiny, evenly spaced stitches.

A visit to the Victorian or needlework departments in museums, or a browse around antique shops, may give inspiration for latter-day knick-knacks which could be made with hairpin crochet.

Looking back

Figure 101 is an example of antique hairpin crochet doylies which were made in profusion around the end of the last century. These can still be found in antique shops, markets and jumble sales. Careful laundering will restore them to their original condition, and will still charm the tea tables of today.

101 An antique doylie.

Looking forward

A close inspection of figure 101 will reveal the fact that more than one round of braid was used; in fact there are four rounds which are joined together with crochet. This represents one aspect of the many other possibilities that hairpin crochet has to offer. There are several methods by which the lengths of hairpin braid can be joined together with further crochet to make wider, more intricate braids and edgings in fine yarn, or complete fabrics can be made by joining several braids together. Wider braids worked in wool produce distinctive open-work items such as scarves, shawls and jackets, to name but a few.

This introduction to hairpin crochet is now complete and there are still many more ways of making and using hairpin braids, edgings and lacy fabrics, but these belong to other books, the titles of which are given in the book list on p.92.

To help you

Taking care of hairpin crochet

Well-made hairpin crochet is hard wearing and will withstand regular washing. Before drying, smooth the braid out with the fingers and it should then only require a light pressing. To care for old hairpin doylies, wash gently by hand, or if there is yellowing with age use a fabric whitener sold for restoring net curtaining to its original brightness. Do not starch as this may make the cotton brittle.

Further reading

Pamela Thompson, *Hairpin Crochet Technique and Design*, 1983
Ena Maidens, *The Techniques of Crocheted and Openwork Lace*, 1982
Ann Stearns, *The Batsford Book of Crochet*, 1981
Jean Kinmond, *The Coats Book of Lacecrafts*, 1978
All are published by Batsford.

The Knitting and Crochet Guild

The Guild was formed in 1978 to foster and develop the crafts of knitting and crochet. It is a lively friendly organisation, its mainstay being a quarterly magazine which supplies lots of information and interesting articles. Visits are arranged to places of interest, occasional day or weekend courses are organised and the Guild often mans a stand at Craft exhibitions around the country. Anyone who is interested in joining should write for details to:
The Crafts Council,
12 Waterloo Place,
London, SW1 Y4AU   Tel: 01 930 4811.

Suppliers

Great Britain

The following offer a postal service. When making enquiries by post, please enclose a stamped addressed envelope.

For hairpins, crochet hooks, perle cotton, and Anchor knitting and crochet yarn:
Pauline Turner,
White Cross,
Lancaster, LA1 4XH   Tel: (0524) 33309

For perle cotton and fine DMC mercerised crochet cotton:
Spinning Jenny,
Bradley,
Keighley,
Yorkshire, BD20 9DD   Tel: (0535) 32469

For a complete range of Coats mercerised crochet cotton, knitting cotton, hairpins, crochet hooks and beads (shop and mail order):
The Handicraft Shop,
47 Northgate,
Canterbury,
Kent, CT1 1BE   Tel: (0227) 51188

For textiles including hessian, huckabak, muslin, embroidery linen:
Limericks (Linens) Ltd,
Limerick House,
117 Victoria Avenue,
Southend-on-Sea,
Essex, SS2 6EL   Tel: (0702) 43486

For lurex yarn (Goldfingering) and Lysbet mercerised cotton, send for a list of local stockists to:
H.G. Twilley Ltd,
Roman Hill,
Stamford,
Lincs., PE9 1BG   Tel: (0780) 52661.

USA

For crochet hooks, hairpins and hairpin looms – Hero stockists, who should be able to order these items.

Mail order stockists for crochet supplies

American Handcrafts, 2617W Seventh Street,
Fort Worth, Texas 76707

Economy Handicrafts, 50–21 69th Street,
Woodside, New York, NY 113077.

Lee Ward, Elgin, Illinois 62120.

Peters Valley Craftsman, Layton, New Jersey
67851.

For a wide range of yarns including perle cotton write for a list
of stockists to:
Coats and Clarke Inc., 42 Park Avenue, New York, NY

Index